1/24     £5

# Harvest

# Harvest

180 RECIPES THROUGH THE SEASONS

PHOTOGRAPHY & ILLUSTRATION
EMILIE GUELPA

**hardie grant** books
MELBOURNE · LONDON

# Contents

# Prawns (shrimp)

## Basil grilled prawns

SERVES
•
2–3

Peel and devein 1 kg (2 lb 3 oz) raw prawns (shrimp) and place in a bowl. Mix together 3 tablespoons extra-virgin olive oil, 2 tablespoons chopped basil and the zest of 1 lemon; season with salt and freshly ground black pepper. Pour over the prawns, cover and marinate in the refrigerator for 40 minutes. Heat a barbecue or heavy-based frying pan or chargrill pan to medium–high. Add the prawns. If barbecuing, cook for 4–5 minutes, turning often until cooked through; if pan-frying, cook for 2–3 minutes each side. Serve with lime wedges and salad.

## Sweet chipotle barbecued prawns

SERVES
•
4

Make a paste by mixing together 3 finely diced chipotles in adobo, 2 crushed garlic cloves, 1 tablespoon brown sugar, zest and juice of 1 lime, 2 teaspoons fish sauce and freshly ground black pepper. Pour over 500 g (1 lb 2 oz) raw prawns (shrimp), peeled and deveined. Mix well to ensure prawns are covered and set aside to marinate for 20 minutes. Cook on a hot barbecue plate or grill for 2–3 minutes on each side and serve with lime wedges.

# Southern fried chicken with 'slaw

This recipe asks for drumsticks, but you can use whatever cut of chicken you like, although the cooking time will vary slightly. The buttermilk, which tenderises the chicken, can be found in most supermarkets. If unavailable, substitute 250 ml (8½ fl oz/1 cup) regular milk mixed with 1 tablespoon of lemon juice. SERVES • 4

8 CHICKEN DRUMSTICKS, SKIN REMOVED

250 ML (8½ FL OZ/I CUP) BUTTERMILK

¼ RED CABBAGE, SHREDDED

4 SPRING ONIONS (SCALLIONS), THINLY SLICED

I GRANNY SMITH APPLE, PEELED AND GRATED

2 TABLESPOONS CHOPPED FLAT-LEAF (ITALIAN) PARSLEY

125 G (4½ OZ/½ CUP) SOUR CREAM

2 TABLESPOONS LEMON JUICE

SALT AND FRESHLY GROUND BLACK PEPPER

85 G (3 OZ/⅔ CUP) CORNFLOUR (CORNSTARCH)

2 TEASPOONS SWEET PAPRIKA

I TEASPOON GROUND CORIANDER

½ TEASPOON CAYENNE PEPPER

I TEASPOON GROUND OREGANO

I TEASPOON GROUND CUMIN

½ TEASPOON GROUND CARDAMOM

2 LITRES (68 FL OZ/8 CUPS) VEGETABLE OIL

LEMON WEDGES, TO SERVE

Put the chicken in a bowl and cover with the buttermilk. Refrigerate for at least 4 hours or overnight.

Preheat the oven to 180°C (350°F).

Put the chicken in a colander to drain the excess buttermilk.

In a large bowl, combine the cabbage, spring onion, apple and parsley. Mix the sour cream and lemon juice together, and season with salt and freshly ground black pepper. Pour over the salad and toss to combine.

In a shallow bowl, mix the cornflour with the spices and 1 teaspoon salt. Dip the chicken pieces into the flour mixture, and shake to remove excess flour.

Heat the oil to 180°C (350°F) in a deep, heavy-based saucepan or deep-fryer.

Deep-fry the chicken, in batches, for 6–8 minutes, until golden. Transfer to the oven and bake for 20 minutes.

Serve with lemon wedges and the 'slaw.

# Zucchini (courgette)

## Spaghetti with zucchini flowers, currants and pine nuts

SERVES
·
4

Boil 400 g (14 oz) spaghetti in salted water for 8 minutes, or until cooked. Meanwhile, heat a splash of oil in a frying pan over medium–high heat. Add 1 finely diced onion and 50 g (1¾ oz/⅓ cup) pine nuts. Cook for 4–5 minutes, stirring often, until the pine nuts turn golden brown. Add 1 crushed garlic clove, 1 seeded and finely chopped small red chilli, the zest of 1 lemon and 12 thinly sliced zucchini (courgette) flowers, and cook for 2–3 minutes, until the vegetables soften. Stir in 80 ml (2½ fl oz/⅓ cup) chicken or vegetable stock and 50 g (1¾ oz/⅓ cup) currants, cover and cook for 1–2 minutes. Check seasoning and add 2 tablespoons chopped flat-leaf (Italian) parsley. Drain the pasta and toss with the sauce.

## Pan-fried zucchini

SERVES
·
4 AS A
LIGHT MEAL

Heat a heavy-based frying pan over medium–high heat. Add a generous splash of oil and 6 zucchini (courgettes) cut into long strips. Cook for 4–5 minutes, tossing often, until the zucchini are golden brown. Remove from the pan and allow to cool. Add a generous amount of salt and freshly ground black pepper along with a handful of roughly torn basil. Add 1 tablespoon white balsamic vinegar and 3 tablespoons extra-virgin olive oil and toss to combine. Serve while still warm with crusty white bread.

# Linguine with mussels cooked in verjuice and saffron

A steaming bowl of mussels makes a great start to any meal; it's also a dish that takes only a few minutes to prepare. Remember to purchase mussels with their shells closed, and discard any that fail to open during cooking. You can serve the mussels in individual portions, but it's more fun to throw them in a big bowl and invite everyone to dive in and share. SERVES • 4

400 G (14 OZ) LINGUINE

OLIVE OIL, FOR FRYING

4 GARLIC CLOVES, CRUSHED

125 ML (4 FL OZ/½ CUP) VERJUICE

PINCH OF SAFFRON THREADS

1 KG (2 LB 3 OZ) MUSSELS, SHELLS SCRUBBED AND BEARDS REMOVED

1 HANDFUL OF FLAT-LEAF (ITALIAN) PARSLEY, CHOPPED

KNOB OF BUTTER

SALT AND FRESHLY GROUND BLACK PEPPER

Bring a large saucepan of water to the boil over high heat. Add a good pinch of salt. Add the linguine and stir until the water has returned to the boil. Reduce the heat, cover and cook the pasta at a fast simmer for 8 minutes.

While the pasta is cooking, heat a wok or large frying pan over high heat. Add a swirl of oil, then the garlic. Stir for 1 minute, or until fragrant. Add the verjuice and saffron. Allow the liquid to come to the boil, then toss in the mussels. Cover with a lid and steam for 3–4 minutes.

Have a large bowl to hand. Remove the lid from the wok, shake the wok well and remove the cooked mussels as they open, placing them directly in the bowl. Check the pasta is cooked, then drain.

Remove the pan from the heat and discard any mussels that didn't open during cooking. Add the parsley and butter to the cooking liquid and whisk through. Check seasoning and add salt and freshly ground black pepper if needed. Pour the cooking juices over the mussels, add the pasta and toss to combine. Serve immediately.

# Blueberry

## Almond, marzipan and blueberry slice

Grease and line the sides and base of a 20 × 30 cm (8 × 12 in) baking tin with baking paper. Cream 100 g (3½ oz) butter and 230 g (8 oz/1 cup) caster (superfine) sugar until light and fluffy. Beat in 2 eggs, one at a time, fully incorporating after each addition. Add ½ teaspoon almond essence. Mix in 225 g (8 oz/1½ cups) plain (all-purpose) flour until just combined. Then stir in 100 g (3½ oz) grated marzipan (chill it in the refrigerator before grating), 80 g (2¾ oz/¾ cup) ground almonds and 155 g (5½ oz/1 cup) fresh blueberries. Spoon into the prepared tin and scatter 45 g (1½ oz/½ cup) flaked almonds over the top. Bake in a preheated 180°C (350°F) oven for 40 minutes, or until a skewer inserted into the slice comes out clean. Allow to cool. Dust with icing (confectioners') sugar and cut into small rectangles.

## Blueberry and coconut muffins

Line eight 125 ml (4 fl oz/½ cup) muffin tins with paper cases and preheat the oven to 180°C (350°F). Cream 100 g (3½ oz) softened butter and 145 g (5 oz/⅔ cup) caster (superfine) sugar until light and fluffy. Add 1 egg and beat until combined. Stir through 125 ml (4 fl oz/½ cup) coconut milk, followed by 200 g (7 oz/1⅓ cups) self-raising flour, 45 g (1½ oz/½ cup) desiccated (shredded) coconut and 100 g (3½ oz) blueberries. Spoon the mix into the prepared muffin tins and top each muffin with a few extra blueberries. Bake for 20 minutes, or until risen and golden brown. Allow to cool, then dust with icing (confectioners') sugar to serve.

## Blueberry crumble cake

To make poached blueberries, bring 125 ml (4 fl oz/½ cup) water and 115 g (4 oz/½ cup) caster (superfine) sugar to the boil. Add 300 g (10½ oz) blueberries, return to the boil and then remove from the heat. Allow to cool.

Preheat the oven to 180°C (350°F) and grease a 23 cm (9 in) round cake tin. Cream together 180 g (6½ oz) softened butter and 145 g (5 oz/⅔ cup) caster (superfine) sugar until light and fluffy. Beat in 2 eggs, one at a time, fully incorporating after each addition. Sift together 150 g (5½ oz/1 cup) self-raising flour and 100 g (3½ oz/⅔ cup) plain (all-purpose) flour, and add to mixture along with 80 ml (2½ fl oz/⅓ cup) milk. Beat until combined. Spoon the mixture into the prepared tin. Scatter with the cooled poached blueberries. Prepare crumble mixture by combining 50 g (1¾ oz/⅓ cup) plain (all-purpose) flour, 60 g (2 oz) butter and 3 tablespoons sugar until the mix forms a breadcrumb texture. Sprinkle the crumble over the fruit then bake for 40–45 minutes, or until a skewer inserted into the cake comes out clean. Allow to cool, then dust with icing (confectioners') sugar.

# Twice-cooked pork belly with cucumber salad and spicy sesame dressing

Is there a better way to start the year than with crispy pork belly transformed into a salad? The cucumber brings contrasting texture, while the spicy sesame dressing takes it to a whole new level. **SERVES • 4**

250 ML (8½ FL OZ/1 CUP) SOY SAUCE

125 ML (4 FL OZ/½ CUP) CHINESE RICE WINE

3–4 SLICES GINGER

1 LEMONGRASS STEM, WHITE PART ONLY, SLICED

2–3 PIECES TANGERINE PEEL (OPTIONAL)

2 STAR ANISE

80 G (2¾ OZ/⅓ CUP) CASTER (SUPERFINE) SUGAR

1 KG (2 LB 3 OZ) PORK BELLY

2 TABLESPOONS LIME JUICE

2 TABLESPOONS FISH SAUCE

1 TABLESPOON HONEY

**CUCUMBER SALAD**

2 LEBANESE (SHORT) CUCUMBERS

15 G (½ OZ/½ CUP) CORIANDER (CILANTRO) LEAVES

6 RED ASIAN SHALLOTS, THINLY SLICED

1 SMALL RED CHILLI, SEEDED AND FINELY CHOPPED

**SPICY SESAME DRESSING**

2 TEASPOONS GRATED GINGER

1 GARLIC CLOVE, CRUSHED

2 SMALL RED CHILLIES, SEEDED AND FINELY CHOPPED

3 TABLESPOONS SOY SAUCE

1 TABLESPOON RICE VINEGAR

2 TEASPOONS TAHINI

1 TABLESPOON SESAME OIL

1 TABLESPOON SESAME SEEDS, TOASTED

Put 1.5 litres (51 fl oz/6 cups) water, the soy sauce, Chinese rice wine, ginger, lemongrass, tangerine peel (if using), star anise and sugar in a large saucepan and bring to the boil. Reduce the heat to low, add the pork belly and simmer for 1½ hours. Remove the saucepan from the heat and allow the pork to cool in the stock for 2–3 hours before transferring the pork to a plate. Refrigerate, uncovered, overnight.

To make the salad, peel the cucumbers, then make long ribbons using a vegetable peeler. Discard the seeds. Put the cucumber ribbons in a colander and leave to drain for 30 minutes. Toss the cucumber with the coriander leaves, Asian shallots and chilli, and set aside until ready to serve.

To make the spicy sesame dressing, mix all of the ingredients together and set aside.

To finish, cut the pork belly into 1 cm (½ in) slices, removing any bones. Combine the lime juice, fish sauce and honey in a small bowl and set aside. Heat a heavy-based frying pan over medium–high heat and dry-fry the pork for 8–10 minutes, stirring often, until golden brown and crispy all over. Drain off any excess fat, add the lime juice mixture and toss to combine.

Toss the spicy sesame dressing through the cucumber salad and arrange on a large platter. Spoon the pork belly over the top and serve immediately.

# Plum

## Roasted plum and marzipan muffins

**MAKES · 12**

Preheat the oven to 180°C (350°F) and grease two six-hole muffin tins. Halve and pit 3 blood plums and place, cut side up, on a lined baking tray. Sprinkle with caster (superfine) sugar and bake for 10–15 minutes, until soft. Set aside to cool. Cream 100 g (3½ oz) softened butter with 115 g (4 oz/½ cup) caster (superfine) sugar until light and fluffy. Beat in 2 eggs, one at a time, fully incorporating after each addition. Mix in 1 teaspoon almond essence and 225 g (8 oz/1½ cups) self-raising flour. Add 100 g (3½ oz) grated marzipan and stir until just combined (chill it in the refrigerator before grating). Roughly chop the plums and fold through the mixture. Spoon into the muffin tins and bake for 20–25 minutes, until risen and golden brown. Allow to cool, then dust with icing (confectioners') sugar.

## Blood plum and amaretti crumble

**SERVES · 6**

Preheat the oven to 180°C (350°F). Make the crumble by roughly crushing 100 g (3½ oz) amaretti biscuits (cookies). In a separate bowl, rub together 2 tablespoons caster (superfine) sugar, 100 g (3½ oz) softened butter, 1 pinch of ground cinnamon and 75 g (2¾ oz/⅓ cup) self-raising flour until the mixture resembles breadcrumbs. Add the crushed amaretti biscuits. Quarter and pit 8 blood plums and put in a saucepan with 80 ml (2½ fl oz/⅓ cup) water and 80 g (2¾ oz/⅓ cup) caster (superfine) sugar and cook over low heat until the plums just start to break down. Stir in 1 teaspoon natural vanilla extract and transfer the stewed plums to a small, deep baking dish. Top with the crumble mixture and cook for 20 minutes, or until golden brown and cooked through. Serve with cream.

## Cinnamon-roasted blood plums with French toast

**SERVES · 4**

Preheat the oven to 180°C (350°F). Halve and pit 4 blood plums, place on a lined baking tray, cut side up, and sprinkle over a mixture of 2 tablespoons caster (superfine) sugar and 1 teaspoon ground cinnamon. Roast for 15–20 minutes, until soft. Whisk 4 eggs, 80 ml (2½ fl oz/⅓ cup) milk and 1 pinch of salt together until combined. Take 4 slices of day-old bread and soak both sides in the egg mixture until all of it is absorbed. Heat a generous splash of oil in a large heavy-based frying pan over medium–high heat. Cook the bread for 3–4 minutes on each side until well browned (you may need to cook in two batches, depending on the size of the bread). Serve immediately with the warm plums, and some maple syrup or honey and yoghurt.

# Seared tuna with fennel confit

Fennel confit has such a lovely rich flavour and beautiful texture, ideally suited to the magnificent tuna fish. You have to cook the fennel long and slow to get the desired texture. SERVES • 4

4 PRESERVED LEMON QUARTERS, PITH DISCARDED AND SKIN THINLY SLICED

80 G (2¾ OZ/½ CUP) PITTED KALAMATA OLIVES, HALVED

I HANDFUL OF FLAT-LEAF (ITALIAN) PARSLEY

4 × 150 G (5½ OZ) TUNA STEAKS

SALT AND FRESHLY GROUND BLACK PEPPER

EXTRA-VIRGIN OLIVE OIL, FOR DRIZZLING

**FENNEL CONFIT**

4 FENNEL BULBS

THINLY SLICED ZEST OF I LEMON

4–6 GARLIC CLOVES

I HANDFUL OF HERBS SUCH AS FLAT-LEAF (ITALIAN) PARSLEY, THYME, ROSEMARY OR SAGE

EXTRA-VIRGIN OLIVE OIL, TO COVER

To make the fennel confit, preheat the oven to 90°C (150°F). Place the fennel in a baking dish or tin so that the fennel fits snugly. Add the lemon zest, garlic and herbs to the fennel and enough olive oil to cover. Cover with foil and cook for 2–3 hours, until tender. Allow to cool, then remove the fennel from the oil and refrigerate until needed.

Lightly toss the preserved lemon, olives and parsley together in a bowl. Halve and core the fennel bulbs, and add to the bowl.

Heat a barbecue grill or chargrill pan until hot. Season the tuna steaks with salt and freshly ground black pepper, and drizzle with olive oil. Rub the oil and seasoning into the fish. Cook the tuna for 1–2 minutes on each side, until it is just seared. Remove and place on individual serving plates. Top each tuna steak with two fennel halves and some of the preserved lemon mixture. Drizzle with extra-virgin olive oil, season with freshly ground black pepper and serve immediately.

# Tomato

## Sticky lemon roast chicken with sweet tomatoes

SERVES
4–6

Preheat the oven to 180°C (350°F). Take either 1.5 kg (3 lb 5 oz) chicken pieces or 1 whole chicken cut into 8 joints and put in a deep baking dish. Add 2 tablespoons olive oil and season with salt and freshly ground black pepper. Add 500 g (1 lb 2 oz) new potatoes (halved if large), 250 g (9 oz) cherry tomatoes, 2 soaked and finely chopped preserved lemon quarters and 1 handful of garlic cloves. Bake for 1 hour, turning occasionally, until the chicken is golden brown and cooked through. Drizzle with the juice of 1 lemon and add 1 handful of roughly chopped flat-leaf (Italian) parsley.

## Tomato tarte tatin

SERVES
4

Cut 4–6 tomatoes (depending on size) in half lengthways. Place on a baking tray, drizzle with olive oil and balsamic vinegar and season with sea salt and freshly ground black pepper. Roast in a preheated 180°C (350°F) oven for 20–30 minutes, or until cooked and golden brown. Grease and line a shallow baking dish or flan (tart) tin with baking paper. Put the tomatoes, cut side down, in the dish, arranging them so they fit snugly. Scatter with caramelised onions or onion jam and 2–3 tablespoons chopped basil. Cover with puff pastry. Bake in a preheated 200°C (400°F) oven for 15–20 minutes, or until the pastry is golden brown. Allow to cool briefly, then place a board or serving plate over the dish and turn upside down, allowing the tart to come out.

## Tomato, pancetta and chickpea soup

SERVES
4

Heat a splash of oil in a large heavy-based saucepan over medium–high heat. Add 1 diced onion, 1 diced carrot and 1 sliced leek and cook for 3–4 minutes, stirring often, until softened. Add 100 g (3½ oz) thick pancetta sliced into batons and cook for 4–5 minutes, until golden brown. Add 1 crushed garlic clove and 1 teaspoon smoked paprika and cook for 1–2 minutes, until fragrant. Add 400 g (14 oz) tinned chopped tomatoes and 750 ml (25½ fl oz/3 cups) chicken stock and bring to the boil. Season and reduce to a simmer and cook for 15–20 minutes. Add 400 g (14 oz) tinned chickpeas (drained and rinsed), check seasoning and finish with 2 tablespoons chopped flat-leaf (Italian) parsley. Delicious with crusty bread and a dollop of pesto.

# Butterflied king prawns with mango and hot mint salsa

Make the most of the summer's mangoes and whip up a delightfully sweet and spicy salsa to complement this refreshing and nutritious combination of barbecued king prawns with rice noodle salad. **SERVES • 6**

24 KING PRAWNS (SHRIMP), SHELLS ON

OIL, FOR COOKING

SALT AND FRESHLY GROUND
BLACK PEPPER

LIME WEDGES, TO SERVE

**MANGO AND HOT MINT SALSA**

1 RIPE MANGO

2 TABLESPOONS LIME JUICE

½ RED ONION, THINLY SLICED

2 SMALL RED CHILLIES, FINELY CHOPPED

1 TABLESPOON SHREDDED
VIETNAMESE MINT

FRESHLY GROUND BLACK PEPPER

1 TABLESPOON FISH SAUCE

To prepare the salsa, peel the mango, remove the flesh from the stone and dice finely. Transfer to a bowl and combine with the lime juice, onion, chilli and Vietnamese mint. Season to taste with freshly ground black pepper and the fish sauce.

To butterfly the prawns, use a sharp knife to slice between the legs from head to tail, taking care not to cut all the way through. Open up the abdomen of one of the prawns and press flat, then discard the intestinal tract and set aside. Repeat with the remaining prawns.

Heat a barbecue grill or chargrill pan until hot. Brush the prawns with oil and cook on the barbecue for 2 minutes on each side, then remove.

Place 4 prawns and a spoonful of mango salsa on individual plates. Serve with lime wedges.

# Broad (fava) beans

## Linguine with broad beans, pancetta and spicy tomato

SERVES
4

First double-pod broad (fava) beans by removing the beans from the large outer pod (you want to end up with a handful of beans). Boil for 1–2 minutes, drain and refresh under cold water. Insert a small knife or your thumbnail into the pale green pod to create a slit, then push the bean out. Bring a large saucepan of salted water to the boil over high heat. Add 400 g (14 oz) linguine and stir until the water returns to the boil. Reduce the heat, cover and cook the pasta for 8 minutes. Heat a splash of oil in a frying pan over medium–high heat, and add 1 finely diced onion and 2 diced thick slices of pancetta. Cook for 4–5 minutes, stirring often, until the pancetta is golden. Add 1 crushed garlic clove, 1 seeded and finely chopped small red chilli and 2 diced vine-ripened tomatoes, and cook for 2–3 minutes, until the tomatoes have softened. Add 80 ml (2½ fl oz/⅓ cup) chicken or vegetable stock, cook for a further 1–2 minutes. Check seasoning, and add the broad beans and 2 tablespoons chopped basil. Drain the pasta and toss with the sauce.

## Radish and broad bean salad

SERVES
4 AS A
SIDE DISH

First double-pod some broad (fava) beans by removing the beans from the large outer pod. Boil for 1–2 minutes, drain and refresh under cold water. Insert a small knife or your thumbnail into the pale green pod to create a slit, then push the bean out (you want to end up with 200 g/7 oz beans). Put the broad beans in a bowl with 200 g (7 oz) sliced radishes, ½ thinly sliced red onion, 2 tablespoons chopped mint, 1 soaked and finely chopped preserved lemon quarter, 1 tablespoon lemon juice, salt and freshly ground black pepper. Drizzle with extra-virgin olive oil and toss to combine. Serve at room temperature.

## Broad bean, preserved lemon and ricotta salad

SERVES
4

First double-pod broad (fava) beans by removing the beans from the large outer pod. Boil for 1–2 minutes, drain and refresh under cold water. Insert a small knife or your thumbnail into the pale green pod to create a slit, then push the bean out (you want to end up with 150 g/5½ oz beans). Blanch 155 g (5½ oz/1 cup) peas and the broad beans until tender. Briefly blanch 4 small zucchini (courgettes) or baby (pattypan) squash and drain well. Cut diagonally into long slices and put in a bowl with the peas and broad beans. Add 200 g (7 oz) tinned chickpeas (drained and rinsed), 25 g (1 oz/⅓ cup) roughly chopped mint, 2 soaked and finely chopped preserved lemon quarters, 1 tablespoon white wine vinegar and 3 tablespoons extra-virgin olive oil. Season well with salt and freshly ground black pepper. Add 400 g (14 oz) crumbled firm ricotta and toss to combine. Delicious for a light lunch, or serve alongside grilled fish or chicken.

# Lamb, fennel and broad bean tagine

Three of early summer's great heroes, together in one dish: the fennel balances the richness of the lamb, while the broad beans speak to the season with their fresh, grassy flavour. SERVES • 6

## SPICE MIXTURE

2 TEASPOONS SWEET PAPRIKA

I TEASPOON GROUND GINGER

I TEASPOON CHILLI POWDER

I TEASPOON GROUND CUMIN

I TEASPOON GROUND CORIANDER

I TEASPOON GROUND WHITE PEPPER

½ TEASPOON GROUND CARDAMOM

½ TEASPOON GROUND CINNAMON

½ TEASPOON GROUND ALLSPICE

I TEASPOON SALT

2 TABLESPOONS LEMON JUICE

3 TABLESPOONS OLIVE OIL, PLUS EXTRA FOR COOKING


I KG (2 LB 3 OZ) DICED LAMB

2 FENNEL BULBS, THINLY SLICED

3 TABLESPOONS ORANGE JUICE

500 ML (17 FL OZ/2 CUPS) CHICKEN STOCK

100 G (3½ OZ) DRIED APRICOTS, DICED

85 G (3 OZ/⅔ CUP) SULTANAS (GOLDEN RAISINS)

I KG (2 LB 3 OZ) BROAD (FAVA) BEANS

30 G (I OZ/I CUP) CORIANDER (CILANTRO) LEAVES

2 TABLESPOONS CHOPPED MINT

4 TABLESPOONS CHOPPED FLAT-LEAF (ITALIAN) PARSLEY

STEAMED COUSCOUS, TO SERVE

TZATZIKI, TO SERVE

Combine the spice mixture ingredients together to form a smooth paste. Coat the diced lamb with the spice mixture and leave to marinate for 4 hours or overnight.

Preheat the oven to 180°C (350°F).

Heat a splash of olive oil in a large heavy-based flameproof casserole dish over medium–high heat and cook the fennel for 5–6 minutes, stirring often, until soft. Remove from the heat, add the marinated lamb, orange juice and stock, cover with a lid and bake in the oven for 1 hour, stirring occasionally. Add the apricots and sultanas and return to the oven, uncovered, for a further 30–60 minutes, until the lamb is tender.

Meanwhile, remove the broad beans from their pods and bring a large saucepan of water to the boil. Cook the beans for 1 minute, then drain and refresh under cold water. Remove the pale green skins by creating a slit in the skin and pushing the beans through it. Discard the skins. Add the broad beans to the tagine in the last 10 minutes of cooking.

Stir through the herbs, check for seasoning and serve with steamed couscous and tzatziki.

# Strawberry

## Strawberry shortbread stack

SERVES
•
6

Preheat the oven to 170°C (340°F). To make shortbread, rub 260 g (9 oz/1¾ cups) plain (all-purpose) flour, 115 g (4 oz/⅔ cup) rice flour, 250 g (9 oz) softened butter, 115 g (4 oz/½ cup) caster (superfine) sugar and a pinch of salt together. When the mixture comes together, turn onto a floured board and knead well to form a dough. Roll out to 5 mm (¼ in) thick and cut 18 circles about 10 cm (4 in) in diameter. Bake the shortbread in the oven until crisp, taking care not to colour the biscuits. Allow to cool before using. Whip 250 ml (8½ fl oz/1 cup) cream to stiff peaks, add 2 tablespoons caster (superfine) sugar and 1 teaspoon natural vanilla extract, and set aside. To serve, place a shortbread on each serving plate, top with cream and sliced strawberries, then top with another shortbread, more cream and strawberries, then a final shortbread on top. Dust with icing (confectioners') sugar.

## Lemon posset with strawberries Romanoff

SERVES
•
4

Bring 500 ml (17 fl oz/2 cups) thick (double/heavy) cream and 115 g (4 oz/½ cup) caster (superfine) sugar to the boil in a saucepan over medium–high heat. Reduce to a simmer and cook for a further 2–3 minutes, stirring constantly. Remove from the heat, add 3 tablespoons lemon juice and stir well. Allow to cool slightly before pouring into four dessert glasses. Refrigerate for at least 4 hours, or until set. To make the strawberries Romanoff, thinly slice 500 g (1 lb 2 oz) strawberries. Mix with 2 tablespoons icing (confectioners') sugar and 2 tablespoons Cointreau or other orange-flavoured liqueur. Leave at room temperature for up to an hour, then serve on top of the lemon posset.

## Chocolate tart with vanilla mascarpone and strawberries

SERVES
•
8

Sift 300 g (10½ oz/2 cups) plain (all-purpose) flour and 2 tablespoons unsweetened cocoa powder together. Rub 150 g (5½ oz) diced butter and 1 pinch of salt into the dry ingredients until the mixture resembles breadcrumbs. In a separate bowl, combine 2 tablespoons caster (superfine) sugar and 1 egg. Add to the flour mixture and mix until the pastry comes together. Wrap in plastic wrap and chill for 30 minutes. On a lightly floured board, roll out the pastry until it is 3 mm (⅛ in) thick. Line a buttered flan (tart) tin with the pastry, using your fingers to push the pastry down into the corners. Trim any excess pastry using a small knife. Preheat the oven to 180°C (350°F) and prick the base of the pastry shell with a fork; refrigerate for 30 minutes. Line the tart shell with baking paper and fill it with pastry weights or uncooked rice. Blind bake for 15 minutes before removing the paper and pastry weights and baking for a further 5 minutes to crisp the pastry. Whip 185 ml (6 fl oz/¾ cup) cream until it forms soft peaks. Combine the seeds from 1 vanilla bean with 150 g (5½ oz) mascarpone and 2 tablespoons icing (confectioners') sugar, then fold through the whipped cream. Before serving, spoon the cream into the cooled pastry shell and arrange 500 g (1 lb 2 oz) strawberries on top.

# Blood plum granita with panna cotta

Most fruits can be made into a granita, but plums, with their inherent tartness and high sugar content, are particularly ideal. SERVES • 6

115 G (4 OZ/½ CUP) CASTER (SUPERFINE) SUGAR

500 G (1 LB 2 OZ) BLOOD PLUMS, CHOPPED

2 TABLESPOONS LEMON JUICE

2 TABLESPOONS FINELY SHREDDED MINT

**PANNA COTTA**

3 × 5 G (¼ OZ) GELATINE LEAVES

500 ML (17 FL OZ/2 CUPS) BUTTERMILK

250 ML (8½ FL OZ/1 CUP) CREAM

1 MINT SPRIG

80 G (2¾ OZ/⅓ CUP) CASTER (SUPERFINE) SUGAR

1 TEASPOON NATURAL VANILLA EXTRACT

To make the panna cotta, soak the gelatine leaves in cold water for 5 minutes, or until softened. Remove from the water and squeeze gently to remove excess liquid before using.

Meanwhile, in a saucepan, bring the buttermilk, cream, mint, sugar and vanilla to the boil. Remove from the heat and briefly allow to cool before adding the gelatine and stirring until dissolved. Strain the liquid then pour into six 125 ml (4 fl oz/½ cup) serving glasses. Refrigerate until set, at least 4 hours or overnight.

For the granita, combine the caster sugar with 125 ml (4 fl oz/½ cup) water in a saucepan over low heat, stirring until dissolved. Bring to the boil, then simmer for 2–3 minutes. Allow to cool.

Put the plums and lemon juice in a food processor and purée until smooth. Strain through a fine-mesh sieve then combine with 100 ml (3½ fl oz) of the cooled sugar syrup and 100 ml (3½ fl oz) water. Pour into a deep rectangular tray and put in the freezer. Every hour, remove the tray from the freezer and scrape into flakes using a fork. Continue until the granita is fluffy and completely frozen. Store in the freezer for up to 3 days, until required.

Stir the shredded mint through the granita, and serve with the panna cottas.

# Raspberry

## Raspberry and pistachio torronata

SERVES
•
8

Mix together 375 g (13 oz) ricotta and 115 g (4 oz/½ cup) caster (superfine) sugar until combined. Whip 250 ml (8½ fl oz/1 cup) cream and incorporate with 150 g (5½ oz) finely chopped nougat, the zest of 1 lemon and 2 tablespoons chopped pistachios. Add 125 g (4½ oz) raspberries and stir through until just combined. Line a loaf (bar) tin with plastic wrap and spoon the ricotta mix in. Cover and freeze for at least 8 hours. Just before serving, remove the torronata from the tin and cut into 1 cm (½ in) slices. Serve with additional raspberries and chopped pistachios.

## Raspberry and white chocolate cake

SERVES
•
8

Preheat the oven to 180°C (350°F), and grease and line a 23 cm (9 in) round cake tin. Melt 160 g (5½ oz) butter with 100 g (3½ oz) white chocolate. In a separate bowl, mix together 300 g (10½ oz/2 cups) self-raising flour and 285 g (10 oz/1¼ cups) caster (superfine) sugar. Whisk in 4 eggs, 1 teaspoon natural vanilla extract, 250 ml (8½ fl oz/1 cup) milk and the melted chocolate mixture until smooth. Fold through 100 g (3½ oz) raspberries and pour into the prepared tin. Bake for 30–40 minutes, or until a skewer inserted into the cake comes out clean. Meanwhile, to make white chocolate ganache, bring 80 ml (2½ fl oz/⅓ cup) cream to the boil. Pour the cream over 150 g (5½ oz) chopped white chocolate and whisk until smooth. When the cake is cool, cover with the white chocolate ganache and fresh raspberries. Dust the cake with icing (confectioners') sugar just before serving.

## Raspberry and chocolate mousse

SERVES
•
6

Gently warm 500 g (1 lb 2 oz/2 cups) crème fraîche in a microwave for 1–2 minutes, stirring every 30 seconds, or stir in a bowl set over a saucepan of simmering water. Melt 200 g (7 oz) chocolate separately in the microwave or over simmering water. Whisk the chocolate into the warm crème fraîche. Pour into six 125 ml (4 fl oz/½ cup) serving dishes or ramekins and top each with 5 or 6 raspberries. Refrigerate for at least 4 hours, until set.

# Almond panna cotta with roasted apricots and amaretti crumble

The appearance of apricots on trees and in markets really signifies the start of summer. Roasting them intensifies their flavour and the almond panna cotta in this recipe adds a delightful contrasting texture. SERVES • 6

**ALMOND PANNA COTTA**

3 × 5 G (¼ OZ) GELATINE LEAVES

375 ML (12½ FL OZ/1½ CUPS) ALMOND MILK

375 ML (12½ FL OZ/1½ CUPS) CREAM

80 G (2¾ OZ/⅓ CUP) CASTER (SUPERFINE) SUGAR

2 TEASPOONS ORANGE-BLOSSOM WATER

6 LARGE APRICOTS

1–2 TABLESPOONS CASTER (SUPERFINE) SUGAR

1–2 TABLESPOONS AMARETTO (OPTIONAL)

75 G (2¾ OZ) AMARETTI BISCUITS (COOKIES)

2 TABLESPOONS SOFT BROWN SUGAR

30 G (1 OZ) BUTTER, DICED

½ TEASPOON GROUND CARDAMOM

MINT LEAVES TO GARNISH

To make the almond panna cotta, soak the gelatine leaves in cold water for 5 minutes, until softened. Remove from the water and squeeze gently to remove excess liquid before using.

Meanwhile, bring the almond milk, cream and caster sugar to the boil. Remove from the heat, add the gelatine and stir well until dissolved. Strain the liquid to remove any lumps, add the orange-blossom water and pour into six 125 ml (4 fl oz/½ cup) dariole moulds. Refrigerate until set, or overnight.

Once the panna cottas have set, preheat the oven to 180°C (350°F). Cut the apricots in half, discarding the stones, and place them, cut side up, on a lined baking tray. Scatter the caster sugar over the top and roast the apricots for 10 minutes to soften them slightly.

Put the amaretti biscuits in a zip-lock bag and crush them with a rolling pin. Transfer them to a bowl and combine with the brown sugar, butter and cardamom. Spoon the amaretti crumble into the warm apricots and return to the oven for a further 15–20 minutes, or until the crumble is crisp and the apricots are cooked.

Meanwhile, remove the panna cottas from the refrigerator and, using a small spatula or knife, work the puddings away from the edge of the moulds. Stand the moulds in boiling water for 4–5 seconds, place a plate on top of each one, then carefully invert so the plate is on the bottom. Gently shake to dislodge the panna cottas.

Serve 2 warm apricot halves alongside each almond panna cotta.

# Mint

## Haloumi fritters with a tomato and mint salsa

MAKES
•
15

To make the tomato and mint salsa, combine 3 finely diced tomatoes, 1 finely diced red onion and 1 tablespoon chopped mint in a bowl. Season with salt and freshly ground black pepper and set aside. Grate 100 g (3½ oz) haloumi and combine with 2 egg yolks, 125 g (4½ oz/½ cup) plain yoghurt and 1 tablespoon chopped mint in a separate large bowl. Sift 150 g (5½ oz/1 cup) self-raising flour, ½ teaspoon baking powder and a pinch of salt, and add to the wet mix. Stir until combined. Whisk 2 egg whites until thick then fold gently into the fritter mix. It should be a nice dropping consistency. Heat a heavy-based frying pan over medium–high heat. Add a 5 mm (¼ in) layer of oil. Fry spoonfuls of the fritter mix until golden brown on both sides and allow to drain on paper towel. Serve with the tomato and mint salsa.

## Cauliflower, mint and chickpea salad

SERVES
•
4

Preheat the oven to 180°C (350°F). Cut ½ cauliflower into florets, toss with olive oil, salt and freshly ground black pepper and roast on a baking tray for 25–30 minutes, until tender and golden. Set aside to cool. Transfer to a bowl and add 150 g (5½ oz) tinned chickpeas (drained and rinsed), 2 tablespoons chopped coriander (cilantro) leaves, 2 tablespoons chopped mint, 3 thinly sliced spring onions (scallions), a handful of baby English spinach leaves and 50 g (1¾ oz/⅓ cup) crumbled feta. Drizzle with extra-virgin olive oil and 1 tablespoon sherry vinegar, season with salt and freshly ground black pepper, and toss to combine.

# Blackcurrant upside-down cheesecake

A twist on your classic cheesecake, turn this luscious dessert upside down and add salty feta to mix things up a bit. SERVES • 6

2 × 5 G (¼ OZ) GELATINE LEAVES

375 ML (12½ FL OZ/1½ CUPS) APPLE JUICE

55 G (2 OZ) COCONUT SUGAR, PLUS
2 TABLESPOONS EXTRA

250 G (9 OZ/2 CUPS) BLACKCURRANTS

80 G (2¾ OZ) BUTTER

110 G (4 OZ/¾ CUP) PLAIN
(ALL-PURPOSE) FLOUR

250 G (9 OZ/1 CUP) CREAM CHEESE,
SOFTENED

1 TEASPOON NATURAL VANILLA EXTRACT

80 G (2¾ OZ/⅓ CUP) CASTER
(SUPERFINE) SUGAR

100 G (3½ OZ) FETA

125 ML (4 FL OZ/½ CUP) WHIPPING CREAM

Soak the gelatine leaves in cold water for 5 minutes, until softened. Remove from the water and squeeze gently to remove excess liquid before using.

Meanwhile, put the apple juice and 2 tablespoons of coconut sugar in a saucepan and bring to the boil. Add the blackcurrants and cook gently for 2–3 minutes. Remove from the heat, add the gelatine and stir well until dissolved.

Divide the blackcurrant jelly between six 200 ml (7 fl oz) glasses and refrigerate until the jelly sets.

Preheat the oven to 180°C (350°F).

Put the butter, flour and remaining 55 g (2 oz) of the coconut sugar in a bowl and rub the butter into the flour until the mixture resembles rough breadcrumbs. Place the crumble mix on a lined baking tray and cook for 12–15 minutes, or until the crumble is golden brown and cooked. Remove from the oven and set aside to cool.

Make the cheesecake mixture by putting the cream cheese, vanilla and caster sugar in a mixing bowl and beating until soft and creamy. Crumble in the feta and fold through. In a separate bowl, whip the cream until stiff peaks form, then fold it through the cheese mixture.

Spoon the cheese filling on top of the blackcurrant jelly and return to the refrigerator until you are ready to serve the cheesecakes. To serve, remove the cheesecakes from the refrigerator. Break up the crumble topping using your fingers and divide it among the glasses; each cake should have at least 2 cm (¾ in) of crumble topping.

# Cherry

## Cherry and almond crostata

SERVES
•
6–8

Make almond pastry by mixing together 300 g (10½ oz/2 cups) plain (all-purpose) flour, 3 tablespoons ground almonds, the zest of 1 lemon and 150 g (5½ oz) diced butter. Blend in a food processor until the mixture resembles breadcrumbs. Add 2–3 tablespoons cold water until the pastry just comes together. Preheat the oven to 180°C (350°F) and grease a 30 cm (12 in) flan (tart) tin or pizza tray. In a separate bowl, combine 155 g (5½ oz/1½ cups) ground almonds, 2 eggs, the zest of 1 lemon and 80 g (2¾ oz/⅓ cup) caster (superfine) sugar. Roll the almond pastry into a 40 cm (16 in) circle. Line the prepared tin or tray with the pastry, allowing the edges to overhang, and prick the base with a fork. Spread the almond mixture over the pastry and top with 500 g (1 lb 2 oz) halved pitted cherries. Fold the overhanging pastry in to enclose the edge of the crostata. Bake for 30–40 minutes, until the pastry is golden brown. Serve warm with cream.

## Cherry ripe sundaes

SERVES
•
4

Make white chocolate ganache by melting 100 g (3½ oz) white chocolate with 3 tablespoons cream. Whisk until smooth and set aside. Make sugar syrup by dissolving 80 g (2¾ oz/⅓ cup) caster (superfine) sugar in 80 ml (2½ fl oz/⅓ cup) water in a saucepan over low heat. Increase the heat and cook for 5–6 minutes, or until it reduces to a light syrup. Add 500 g (1 lb 2 oz) pitted and halved cherries, bring to the boil then remove from the heat. Drain the cherries and reserve the syrup. Toast 20 g (¾ oz/⅓ cup) shredded coconut until golden brown. In four tall glasses, layer vanilla ice cream, the white chocolate ganache, cherries and toasted coconut. Drizzle with the reserved syrup.

## Cherry ripe cake

SERVES
•
6–8

First, make poached cherries by stirring 230 g (8 oz/1 cup) caster (superfine) sugar and 500 ml (17 fl oz/2 cups) water in a saucepan over low heat until the sugar dissolves. Bring to the boil then add 500 g (1 lb 2 oz) pitted cherries. Cook briefly then drain. Preheat the oven to 180°C (350°F) and grease a 23 cm (9 in) round cake tin. Cream 185 g (6½ oz) softened butter with 230 g (8 oz/1 cup) caster (superfine) sugar until light and fluffy. Beat in 3 eggs, one at a time, fully incorporating after each addition. Sift together 225 g (8 oz/1½ cups) self-raising flour and 60 g (2 oz/½ cup) unsweetened cocoa powder, and add to the mix along with 45 g (1½ oz/½ cup) desiccated (shredded) coconut. Beat well to combine. Stir in 125 g (4½ oz/½ cup) sour cream and half the poached cherries. Spoon into the tin and bake for 40 minutes, or until a skewer inserted into the cake comes out clean. Allow to cool completely. To make ganache, put 250 g (9 oz/1⅓ cups) chopped dark chocolate in a bowl. Bring 125 ml (4 fl oz/½ cup) cream to the boil then pour over the chocolate. Stir until smooth. Top the cake with the ganache and the remaining cherries. Garnish with toasted coconut flakes.

# Summer mango trifle

Traditionally trifle is made of layers of sponge, jelly, fruit and cream, but there's no reason we can't mix it up a bit. **SERVES • 6–8**

1 MANGO, PEELED, STONE REMOVED AND SLICED

100 G (3½ OZ) SPONGE CAKE PIECES

2 EGG YOLKS

2 TABLESPOONS CASTER (SUPERFINE) SUGAR

1 TABLESPOON PLAIN (ALL-PURPOSE) FLOUR

500 ML (17 FL OZ/2 CUPS) MILK

WHIPPED CREAM, TO SERVE

PISTACHIO SLIVERS, FOR SCATTERING

**JELLY**

115 G (4 OZ/½ CUP) CASTER (SUPERFINE) SUGAR

2 × 5 G (¼ OZ) GELATINE LEAVES

250 ML (8½ FL OZ/1 CUP) MANGO JUICE OR MANGO PURÉE

Make the jelly by placing the sugar in a small saucepan with 250 ml (8½ fl oz/1 cup) water and cook over low heat to dissolve the sugar. Increase the heat and bring to the boil, then add the gelatine leaves, remove from the heat and stir until the gelatine dissolves.

Add the mango juice or purée. Pour the jelly mix into a trifle bowl, or individual bowls if preferred, then refrigerate. When set, top with half the mango slices, then the sponge cake pieces.

Make a custard by beating the egg yolks with the caster sugar until pale. Add the flour and combine. Bring the milk to the boil in a saucepan, then pour over the egg mixture and stir to combine. Return the mixture to the saucepan and place over low heat, stirring regularly as the custard thickens, until it comes to the boil. Remove from the heat and leave to cool.

Once cool, spoon the custard over the sponge cake pieces and finish with whipped cream, the rest of the fresh mango and pistachio slivers.

# Panettone and raspberry pudding with marinated cherries

Panettone is a wonderful gift to give or receive around Christmas time and is delicious served with a glass of sweet wine. This recipe is a marvellous way to use up any leftover panettone. It's a simple and lighter twist on a bread and butter pudding, with bursts of flavour from the raspberries and cherries. SERVES • 8

500 G (1 LB 2 OZ) CHERRIES, PITTED AND HALVED

1 TABLESPOON GRAND MARNIER

10 SLICES PANETTONE (APPROXIMATELY 500 G/1 LB 2 OZ)

150 G (5½ OZ) FRESH OR FROZEN RASPBERRIES

3 EGGS

3 TABLESPOONS CASTER (SUPERFINE) SUGAR

500 ML (17 FL OZ/2 CUPS) MILK

1 TEASPOON NATURAL VANILLA EXTRACT

2 TABLESPOONS FLAKED ALMONDS

1–2 TABLESPOONS CASTER (SUPERFINE) SUGAR, ADDITIONAL FOR TOPPING

500 ML (17 FL OZ/2 CUPS) CREAM, TO SERVE

Preheat the oven to 180°C (350°F).

Combine the cherry halves with the Grand Marnier and leave to infuse.

Generously butter a pie dish and arrange the panettone slices so that they overlap each other. Scatter the raspberries over the top.

Beat the eggs, caster sugar, milk and vanilla together in a bowl, then pour over the panettone slices. Allow to stand for 10–15 minutes, then gently push the panettone down to soak up the egg custard mixture. Scatter the flaked almonds and additional caster sugar over the top.

Bake for 40–45 minutes, until the pudding is puffed and golden.

Spoon the marinated cherries on top of the pudding and serve immediately with cream.

# Peach

## Peach crumble cake

SERVES
•
8

Grease and line a 23 cm (9 in) round cake tin and preheat the oven to 180°C (350°F). Cream 180 g (6½ oz) softened butter and 145 g (5 oz/⅔ cup) caster (superfine) sugar until light and fluffy. Add 2 eggs, one at a time, fully incorporating after each addition. Add 250 g (9 oz/1⅔ cups) self-raising flour and 80 ml (2½ fl oz/⅓ cup) milk. Beat until combined. Spoon the mix into the prepared tin and arrange 3 sliced peaches on top. Combine 50 g (1¾ oz/⅓ cup) plain (all-purpose) flour, 60 g (2 oz) diced butter, 75 g (2¾ oz/⅓ cup) raw (demerara) sugar and 1 teaspoon ground cinnamon until the mixture resembles breadcrumbs. Stir through 45 g (1½ oz/½ cup) flaked almonds, then sprinkle the crumble mixture over the cake. Bake for 40–45 minutes, or until a skewer inserted into the cake comes out clean. Allow to cool, then dust with icing (confectioners') sugar to serve.

## Peach and star anise chutney

MAKES
•
1.25 LITRES
(42 FL OZ/5 CUPS)

Bring 125 ml (4 fl oz/½ cup) white wine vinegar to the boil with 95 g (3¼ oz/½ cup lightly packed) soft brown sugar, 1 finely diced onion and 3–4 whole star anise. Continue to boil until the liquid is reduced by half. Thinly slice 8 peaches and add the slices to the syrup. Stir until the syrup returns to the boil. Reduce to a simmer and cook for a further 20 minutes, or until thick and syrupy. Remove from the heat and pour into sterilised glass jars.

# Eton mess

Eton mess is the quintessential summer dessert. Macerating the strawberries in a little berry liqueur gives it that extra pop of flavour. SERVES • 6

750 G (1 LB 11 OZ) STRAWBERRIES, HULLED AND CUT INTO THICK SLICES

2 TABLESPOONS BERRY LIQUEUR OR COINTREAU, PLUS EXTRA TO TASTE

ICING (CONFECTIONERS') SUGAR, FOR DUSTING

250 ML (8½ FL OZ/1 CUP) WHIPPING CREAM

250 G (9 OZ/1 CUP) PLAIN YOGHURT

6 PLAIN MERINGUE NESTS

Put all but 200 g (7 oz) of the strawberries in a bowl and sprinkle with the liqueur. Dust with icing sugar and chill for 1–2 hours.

Whiz the remaining berries into a purée, adding liqueur to taste, and chill.

In the bowl of an electric mixer, beat the cream to soft peaks, fold in the yoghurt and chill.

Roughly crush the meringue nests into bite-sized pieces. When ready to serve, gently toss the cream mixture, meringue and strawberries and pile it into a glass bowl. Drizzle with the strawberry purée.

Toss once and then serve.

# Raspberry and goat's curd filo tart

A luscious combination of fragrant berries, tangy goat's curd and delicate pastry, this impressive tart is surprisingly simple to make. SERVES • 6–8

10–12 SHEETS FILO PASTRY

MELTED BUTTER, FOR BRUSHING

250 G (9 OZ) GOAT'S CURD

115 G (4 OZ/½ CUP) CASTER (SUPERFINE) SUGAR

3 EGGS

1 TEASPOON NATURAL VANILLA EXTRACT

125 G (4½ OZ/½ CUP) PLAIN YOGHURT

ZEST OF 1 LEMON

150 G (5½ OZ) RASPBERRIES

Preheat the oven to 180°C (350°F). Grease a 24 cm (9½ in) flan (tart) tin.

Cut the filo pastry into squares slightly larger than the tart tin. Brush each sheet of filo with butter and line the tin with them.

In a bowl, whisk together the goat's curd, sugar, eggs, vanilla, yoghurt and lemon zest.

Spoon the mixture into the pastry-lined tin. Scatter the raspberries over the top and bake for 30–40 minutes, until firm. Allow to cool before cutting and serving.

# Pear

## Toffee pear galettes

SERVES
•
4

Make dulce de leche by simmering a tin of unopened condensed milk in a saucepan of water, ensuring the tin stays covered with water at all times, for 2½ hours. Remove from the water and allow to cool at room temperature before opening. Preheat the oven to 200°C (400°F). Cut 1 puff pastry sheet into 4 squares and arrange on a lined baking tray. Put a spoonful of dulce de leche in the centre of each piece. Top each dollop with half a thinly sliced pear. Brush the edges of the puff pastry with egg wash and bake for 15–18 minutes, or until the pastry is golden brown and cooked through. Serve with crème fraîche.

## Pear and chocolate crumble

SERVES
•
4–6

Peel, core and dice 6 pears. Put in a saucepan with zest and juice of 1 lemon, 3 tablespoons caster (superfine) sugar and just enough water to cover. Bring to the boil, reduce to a simmer and cook for 10 minutes. Allow to cool slightly. Rub together 150 g (5½ oz) softened diced butter and 250 g (9 oz/1⅔ cups) plain (all-purpose) flour until it forms a breadcrumb texture. Add 140 g (5 oz/¾ cup lightly packed) soft brown sugar, 50 g (1¾ oz) chopped roasted hazelnuts and 50 g (1¾ oz/½ cup) rolled (porridge) oats. Put the pears with a little of the cooking liquid in a baking dish. Sprinkle over 100 g (3½ oz/⅔ cup) chopped chocolate, followed by the crumble mixture. Bake in a preheated 180°C (350°F) oven for 20–25 minutes, until golden brown. Serve with cream.

## Pear and almond tart

SERVES
•
8

To make sweetcrust pastry, sift 200 g (7 oz/1⅓ cups) plain (all-purpose) flour with a pinch of salt, and rub in 125 g (4½ oz) softened diced butter to produce a breadcrumb texture. Add enough water to bring the dough together (2–3 tablespoons) and knead briefly. Wrap in plastic wrap and chill for 30 minutes before use. Preheat the oven to 180°C (350°F). On a lightly floured board, roll out the pastry until it is 3 mm (⅛ in) thick. Line a buttered 25 cm (10 in) flan (tart) tin with the pastry, using your fingers to push the pastry down into the edges. Line the pastry with baking paper and fill it with pastry weights or uncooked rice. Blind bake for 15 minutes before removing the paper and pastry weights or rice. Meanwhile, bring 250 ml (8½ fl oz/1 cup) water and 230 g (8 oz/1 cup) caster (superfine) sugar to the boil in a saucepan over medium heat. Reduce the heat and simmer for 5 minutes. Peel, quarter and core 3 pears and poach them in the sugar syrup for 5–10 minutes, until soft. Drain the pears and set aside. Beat 3 eggs together with 115 g (4 oz/ ½ cup) caster (superfine) sugar, ½ teaspoon almond essence, 100 g (3½ oz/1 cup) ground almonds and 250 g (9 oz) ricotta. Put the pear quarters in the sweetcrust pastry shell and spoon the almond mixture over. Bake for 20–25 minutes in the preheated oven, until golden. Serve warm with cream.

# Pan-fried fish with beetroot and pear salad

Add an additional wow factor to this dish by using golden or candy-striped Chioggia beetroot. Try browsing your local farmers' market for more options. SERVES • 4

4 BEETROOT (BEETS)

3 LEMONS

SALT AND FRESHLY GROUND BLACK PEPPER

3 TABLESPOONS EXTRA-VIRGIN OLIVE OIL

4 TABLESPOONS THINLY SLICED MINT

3 FIRM PEARS

3 TABLESPOONS LEMON JUICE

OIL, FOR COOKING

4 × 150 G (5½ OZ) FIRM WHITE FISH FILLETS, SUCH AS BLUE-EYE TREVALLA

LEMON WEDGES, TO SERVE

To make the salad, peel the beetroot and use a food processor to shred them into long, thin strips. Not only will this save time, but it will also prevent the kitchen and your hands from turning pink. If you don't have a food processor, cut the beetroot into long, thin matchsticks. Put in a large bowl and set aside.

Remove the skin from the lemons with a sharp knife, cutting away the peel and bitter white pith. Using a small bowl to catch any juice, cut between the membranes to remove each lemon segment, adding them to the beetroot as you go. Squeeze any remaining juice from the membranes into the small bowl, season the lemon juice with salt and freshly ground black pepper and add the olive oil. Set aside until ready to serve.

Add the mint to the beetroot and lemon segments and toss to combine.

Prepare the pears just before serving to prevent it from discolouring. Slice the cheeks off the pears, leaving the cores behind. Cut each cheek into thin slices, and then cut each slice into long, thin matchsticks. Once cut, toss with the 3 tablespoons of lemon juice to prevent discolouration.

Heat a heavy-based frying pan over medium–high heat. Add a generous splash of oil and cook each piece of fish for 5–6 minutes, or until golden brown on one side and cooked almost halfway through. Turn the fish over and cook for a further 4–5 minutes, or until the flesh is opaque and flakes easily. If necessary, you may need to use two pans or cook the fish in batches. Do not overcrowd the pan or the fish will not cook properly.

To serve, add the pear to the beetroot salad and toss to combine. Dress with the lemon dressing and check for seasoning. Divide the fish and salad between the serving plates, add lemon wedges and serve immediately.

# Lime

## Scallops with lime and wasabi butter

SERVES
•
2–4

Search out a good fishmonger who sells scallops on the shell with the vivid orange roe still attached. Put 250 g (9 oz) softened butter in a bowl. Add freshly ground black pepper, the zest of 1 lime and 3 teaspoons wasabi paste. Mix well until combined. Turn the butter out onto a square of baking paper and form a sausage shape. Roll up and put in the freezer. Place 24 scallops on the half-shell on a baking tray and cook under a hot grill (broiler) for 2–3 minutes. Remove from the grill, add thin slices of lime and wasabi butter to each scallop and serve.

## Pan-fried fish with lime butter and bok choy

SERVES
•
4

Mix together 100 g (3½ oz) softened butter, the zest of 1 lime, salt and freshly ground black pepper. Roll into a log shape and refrigerate. Heat a splash of olive oil in a heavy-based frying pan over medium–high heat and add a spoonful of butter. Cook 600 g (1 lb 5 oz) firm white fish fillets, in batches, for 3–4 minutes on each side, until golden and cooked through. Cut 6 bok choy (pak choy) in half lengthways, blanch in a saucepan of boiling water for 2–3 minutes, until just cooked. Drain and dress with a splash of soy sauce and a squeeze of lime. Top the fish with slices of the lime butter to serve.

## Lime salmon skewers

SERVES
•
4

Mix together 1 tablespoon soy sauce, the zest of 1 lime, 2 tablespoons chopped coriander (cilantro) leaves and 2 tablespoons chopped mint. Season with freshly ground black pepper. Remove the skin from 4 salmon fillets and cut the fillets into 2 cm (¾ in) cubes. Pour the marinade over the fish and marinate for 20 minutes. Thread 4 pieces of fish onto each skewer. Cook on a hot barbecue for 3–4 minutes on each side, drizzling with oil as needed.

# Chipotle chicken tenders with lime aïoli and coriander salsa

This recipe can be adapted to use most cuts of chicken. If using larger pieces or meat on the bone, you may need to finish cooking the fried chicken in a preheated oven to ensure it is cooked through. SERVES • 6

500 ML (17 FL OZ/2 CUPS) BUTTERMILK

SALT AND FRESHLY GROUND
BLACK PEPPER

I KG (2 LB 3 OZ) CHICKEN TENDERLOINS

300 G (10½ OZ/2 CUPS) PLAIN
(ALL-PURPOSE) FLOUR

2 TEASPOONS CHIPOTLE CHILLI POWDER

2 TABLESPOONS CHOPPED CORIANDER
(CILANTRO)

OIL, FOR FRYING

**LIME AÏOLI**

4 EGG YOLKS

2 TABLESPOONS LIME JUICE

2 GARLIC CLOVES

I TEASPOON DIJON MUSTARD

SALT AND FRESHLY GROUND
BLACK PEPPER

250 ML (8½ FL OZ/1 CUP) OLIVE OIL

I–2 TABLESPOONS BOILING WATER

**CORIANDER SALSA**

2 TABLESPOONS CAPERS, RINSED
AND CHOPPED

30 G (1 OZ/1 CUP) ROUGHLY CHOPPED
FLAT-LEAF (ITALIAN) PARSLEY

60 G (2 OZ/2 CUPS) CORIANDER
(CILANTRO) LEAVES

2 LEMONS

2 TABLESPOONS OLIVE OIL

SALT AND FRESHLY GROUND
BLACK PEPPER

To make the lime aïoli, put the egg yolks, lime juice, garlic and mustard in the bowl of a food processor. Season with salt and freshly ground black pepper. Process for 5 minutes, or until pale and doubled in volume. With the motor still running, slowly drizzle in the olive oil, taking care not to let the egg yolks curdle. Finish with enough boiling water to achieve your preferred consistency. Store in the refrigerator; this can be made up to 1 week in advance.

Put the buttermilk in a large bowl and season well with salt and freshly ground black pepper. Add the chicken tenderloins and leave them to marinate in the refrigerator for up to 4 hours.

Prepare the coriander salsa by mixing the capers, parsley, coriander and the zest of 1 lemon in a bowl. Remove the peel and pith from both lemons with a sharp knife and cut between the membranes to remove each segment, reserving any juice. Stir the lemon segments through the salsa. Whisk the reserved juice with the oil in a separate bowl, season with salt and pepper and set aside.

In a separate bowl, combine the flour, chipotle chilli powder and coriander. Season well with salt and freshly ground black pepper.

Heat 4 cm (1½ in) of oil in a wok or deep saucepan. The oil is hot enough for frying when a cube of bread dropped into the oil turns brown in 20 seconds. Dredge each tenderloin in the flour mixture, then dip in the buttermilk and dredge again in the flour mixture. Gently lower 4–5 chicken pieces (depending on the size of your saucepan) into the hot oil and cook until golden, turning the tenderloins over once. Remove with a slotted spoon, drain on paper towel and sprinkle with salt.

Dress the coriander salsa with the lemon dressing. Serve the chicken with the salsa and lime aïoli.

# Mushroom

## Mushroom and freekeh salad

SERVES
•
4–6

Heat 2 tablespoons olive oil in a saucepan over medium heat. Cook 1 diced onion for 3–4 minutes, then add 85 g (3 oz/½ cup) freekeh and 170 ml (5½ fl oz/⅔ cup) water and bring to the boil. Reduce to a simmer and cook for 10 minutes, or until the liquid has been absorbed and the freekeh is tender. Heat a generous splash of oil in a large frying pan over medium heat. Add 500 g (1 lb 2 oz) mixed mushrooms (Swiss brown, oyster and shiitake), season with freshly ground black pepper and cook for 5–6 minutes, stirring often. Add 2–3 tablespoons stock or water and 2 tablespoons soy sauce, cover with a lid and cook for a further 5 minutes. Transfer to a bowl and allow to cool. Combine the freekeh and mushrooms, season well, then dress with 3 tablespoons chopped flat-leaf (Italian) parsley, 1 tablespoon lemon juice and 2 tablespoons olive oil.

## Polenta with mushrooms and parmesan

SERVES
•
4 AS A
SIDE DISH

Preheat the oven to 180°C (350°F). Bring 500 ml (17 fl oz/2 cups) water and 500 ml (17 fl oz/2 cups) stock to the boil in a heavy-based saucepan. Sprinkle in 150 g (5½ oz/1 cup) polenta and whisk. Reduce to a low simmer and cook for 10–15 minutes, stirring often. Remove from the heat and stir in 75 g (2¾ oz/¾ cup) grated parmesan. Season with salt and freshly ground black pepper, and pour into a baking dish. Heat a splash of oil in a heavy-based frying pan over medium–high heat. Add 500 g (1 lb 2 oz) mixed mushrooms cut into even-sized pieces. Season with salt and pepper and cook for 4–5 minutes, stirring often. Add 2 tablespoons chopped flat-leaf (Italian) parsley and 1 tablespoon chopped basil. Spread the mushrooms over the polenta and top with 50 g (1¾ oz/½ cup) shaved parmesan. Bake for 30 minutes, or until golden brown.

## Pan-fried mushrooms with soy and butter

SERVES
•
4–6 AS A
SIDE DISH

Cut 300 g (10½ oz) mixed mushrooms into even-sized pieces. Heat a splash of olive oil in a heavy-based frying pan over medium–high heat. Sauté the mushrooms for 5–6 minutes, stirring often. Add 1 tablespoon butter and stir to coat. Add 1 tablespoon soy sauce, freshly ground black pepper and a handful of chopped herbs, such as flat-leaf (Italian) parsley and basil, and toss to combine. Serve immediately. Delicious with grilled steak.

# Braised chicken with mushrooms, pancetta and soft polenta

This classic autumn dish uses mushrooms at their prime. The smoky richness of the pancetta transforms otherwise humble ingredients. SERVES • 4–6

OLIVE OIL, FOR COOKING

I ONION, DICED

125 G (4½ OZ) THICKLY SLICED PANCETTA, DICED

600 G (I LB 5 OZ) BONELESS, SKINLESS CHICKEN THIGHS, DICED

2 TABLESPOONS PLAIN (ALL-PURPOSE) FLOUR

250 G (9 OZ) FIELD MUSHROOMS, SLICED

2 CARROTS, CUT INTO CHUNKS

125 ML (4 FL OZ/½ CUP) WHITE WINE

250 ML (8½ FL OZ/I CUP) TOMATO PASSATA (PURÉED TOMATOES)

500–750 ML (17–25½ FL OZ/2–3 CUPS) CHICKEN STOCK

SALT AND FRESHLY GROUND BLACK PEPPER

2–3 THYME SPRIGS

2–3 BAY LEAVES

2 TABLESPOONS CHOPPED FLAT-LEAF (ITALIAN) PARSLEY

**SOFT POLENTA**

500 ML (17 FL OZ/2 CUPS) CHICKEN OR VEGETABLE STOCK

180 G (6½ OZ) POLENTA

60 G (2 OZ) PARMESAN, GRATED OR SHAVED

Heat a splash of oil in a large heavy-based saucepan over a medium–high heat. Cook the onion for 3–4 minutes, then add the pancetta and cook for another 3–4 minutes, stirring often, until it starts to turn golden brown. Add the chicken and cook for 4–5 minutes, until golden brown. Lower the heat, add the flour and cook for 2–3 minutes, stirring occasionally. Add the mushroom, carrot, wine, tomato passata and enough stock to just cover. Season with salt and freshly ground black pepper, then add the thyme and bay leaves. Bring to the boil, reduce to a simmer, cover and cook for 30–35 minutes, stirring occasionally, until the chicken is cooked through.

Meanwhile, to make the polenta, after simmering the chicken for 15 minutes bring 500 ml (17 fl oz/ 2 cups) water and the stock to the boil in another heavy-based saucepan. Sprinkle in the polenta and stir constantly with a long-handled spoon to prevent lumps from forming. Reduce the heat to low and gently simmer for 10–15 minutes, stirring often, until the polenta thickens. Take care, as the polenta can spatter and burn. Remove from the heat, stir in the parmesan and season to taste.

To serve, divide the polenta among serving bowls and spoon over the braised chicken and mushroom mixture.

# Carrot

## Asian chicken 'slaw

SERVES
•
4

Thinly shred ½ Chinese cabbage (wombok) and put in a large bowl. Peel long thin strips from 2 carrots and 1 peeled cucumber and put in the bowl with the cabbage. Add 1 handful of chopped coriander (cilantro) and 1 handful of bean sprouts. Add the shredded flesh from a barbecued chicken and toss together. Make a dressing by combining the juice and zest of 1 lime, 1 teaspoon palm sugar (jaggery) and 2 teaspoons rice vinegar in a bowl. Stir until the sugar dissolves. Add 2 teaspoons fish sauce and 1 tablespoon sweet chilli sauce. Toss the 'slaw with the dressing when ready to serve.

## Baked fish parcels with carrot, coconut milk and kaffir lime

SERVES
•
4

Cut long strips from a carrot using a vegetable peeler. Cut 3 baby bok choy (pak choy) into bite-sized pieces. Lay four baking paper squares out flat. Divide the carrot and bok choy among the squares and lay 1 kaffir lime leaf on top of each pile. Divide 2 sliced spring onions (scallions) and 1 sliced lemongrass stem (white part only) among the piles. Sprinkle with fish sauce. Place a piece of white fish on top of each and add 1 tablespoon coconut milk to each parcel. Fold the paper ends in and pull the remaining two edges up together. Roll over tightly to finish on top of the fish. Cook the fish in a preheated 180°C (350°F) oven for 15 minutes. Serve with jasmine rice.

## Tofu and vegetable laksa

SERVES
•
4

Soak 200 g (7 oz) rice noodles in boiling water for 4–5 minutes, or until the noodles soften. Drain and set aside. Heat 2 tablespoons oil in a large saucepan or wok over medium heat. Fry 2 tablespoons laksa paste for 2–3 minutes, or until aromatic. Add 500 ml (17 fl oz/2 cups) chicken or vegetable stock, 250 ml (8½ fl oz/1 cup) water and 400 ml (13½ fl oz) coconut milk and bring to the boil. Add 1 tablespoon fish sauce, ½ sliced red capsicum (bell pepper), 1 julienned carrot and 200 g (7 oz) chopped broccolini. Simmer for 4–5 minutes. To serve, divide the noodles among four bowls. Add some bean sprouts and slices of tofu. Ladle the broth into the bowls and top with 1 large handful of herbs and crisp-fried shallots. Serve with lime wedges.

# Pepper-crusted beef fillet with horseradish potatoes and beetroot

This spicy crusted beef is an autumn delight, with roasted baby beetroots and creamy potatoes. Look for new potatoes such as pink eyes or nicolas. **SERVES • 4–6**

2 TEASPOONS BLACK PEPPERCORNS

2 GARLIC CLOVES

1 TEASPOON SALT

3 TABLESPOONS FINELY GRATED HORSERADISH

2–3 TABLESPOONS OLIVE OIL

1 × 600 G (1 LB 5 OZ) EYE FILLET STEAK

8 BABY BEETROOT (BEETS), TRIMMED

SALT AND FRESHLY GROUND BLACK PEPPER

1 KG (2 LB 3 OZ) NEW POTATOES

250 G (9 OZ/1 CUP) CRÈME FRAÎCHE OR SOUR CREAM

2 TABLESPOONS CHOPPED FLAT-LEAF (ITALIAN) PARSLEY

Preheat the oven to 180°C (350°F).

Toast the peppercorns in a dry frying pan over medium heat for 1–2 minutes. Crush using a mortar and pestle. Add the garlic cloves and the 1 teaspoon of salt to the bowl of the mortar and pound until smooth. Mix in 2 teaspoons of the horseradish and enough olive oil to form a smooth paste.

Heat 2 tablespoons of the olive oil in a heavy-based frying pan over medium–high heat. Sear the beef for 2–3 minutes on all sides, until golden brown. Rub the pepper paste over the seared beef and place on a baking tray. Scatter the beetroot around the beef, and season with salt and freshly ground black pepper. Roast for 25 minutes, or until the beef is cooked to your liking (medium-rare is ideal). Remove the beef from the oven, cover with foil and rest in a warm place for 8–10 minutes. Check to see if the beetroot are cooked. If not, return to the oven and continue cooking.

Meanwhile, put the potatoes in a saucepan, cover with cold water and bring to the boil. Reduce to a simmer and cook for 20–25 minutes, until tender. Drain, put in a large bowl and remove the skins if desired. While the potatoes are still hot, mash roughly, keeping the potatoes quite chunky. In a separate bowl, mix the crème fraîche or sour cream with the parsley and the remaining horseradish, and season well with salt and freshly ground black pepper. Mix through the mashed potato. To serve, carve the beef into thick slices and serve with the potatoes and roasted beetroot.

# Corn

## Barbecued corn salsa

SERVES
•
4 AS A
SIDE DISH

Remove the husks from 3 corn cobs and pull off the silky tassels. Brush the corn with oil, season with salt and freshly ground black pepper and cook over a hot barbecue grill or chargrill pan, until slightly blackened. Using a sharp knife, slice the kernels away from the corn cob and add to a bowl along with 1 thinly sliced green chilli, 50 g (1¾ oz/1 cup) chopped coriander (cilantro), 2 tablespoons lime juice, 3 tablespoons olive oil and ½ thinly sliced red onion. Season with salt and freshly ground black pepper and mix to combine. Serve over the top of pan-fried fish.

## Cheesy corn and polenta wedges

SERVES
•
4

Bring 500 ml (17 fl oz/2 cups) water and 500 ml (17 fl oz/2 cups) chicken stock to the boil in a heavy-based saucepan. Sprinkle in 150 g (5½ oz/1 cup) polenta, whisking well to prevent lumps forming. Reduce to a low simmer and cook for 20 minutes, stirring often, until the mixture thickens. Take care, as the hot polenta can spatter; a long-handled spoon is ideal. Add more stock or water if it becomes too thick to stir. Remove from the heat and stir in 75 g (2¾ oz/¾ cup) grated parmesan, 4 thinly sliced spring onions (scallions) and corn kernels from 2 corn cobs. Season to taste, then pour the cooked polenta into a deep baking dish and allow to set for at least 4 hours. Preheat the oven to 180°C (350°F). Cut the polenta into wedges or triangles. Arrange the wedges on an oiled baking tray and bake for 20 minutes, or until crisp and golden.

# Sichuan salt and pepper quail with Asian greens

Most good butchers sell quails already spatchcocked. If not, just ask — they are usually happy to help. **SERVES** • 6

250 ML (8½ FL OZ/1 CUP) SOY SAUCE

125 ML (4 FL OZ/½ CUP) CHINESE RICE WINE

3–4 SLICES GINGER

1 LEMONGRASS STEM, WHITE PART ONLY, SLICED

2–3 PIECES TANGERINE PEEL (OPTIONAL)

2 STAR ANISE

80 G (2¾ OZ/⅓ CUP) CASTER (SUPERFINE) SUGAR

6 QUAIL, SPATCHCOCKED (ASK YOUR BUTCHER TO DO THIS)

2 TABLESPOONS SICHUAN PEPPERCORNS

3 TABLESPOONS SEA SALT

OIL, FOR COOKING

LIME WEDGES, TO SERVE

**ASIAN GREENS**

200 G (7 OZ) CHINESE BROCCOLI (GAI LAN)

OIL, FOR COOKING

2 GARLIC CLOVES, CRUSHED

1 TABLESPOON GRATED GINGER

200 G (7 OZ) BROCCOLINI, CUT INTO 2 CM (¾ IN) LENGTHS

80 ML (2½ FL OZ/⅓ CUP) CHICKEN STOCK

1–2 TABLESPOONS SOY SAUCE

Begin this recipe the day before. Prepare a master stock by bringing 1.5 litres (51 fl oz/6 cups) water, the soy sauce, rice wine, ginger, lemongrass, tangerine peel (if using), star anise and sugar to the boil in a large saucepan. Reduce the heat to just below simmering, add the quail and cook for 10 minutes, making sure the liquid doesn't boil. Remove the quail and allow to cool before laying them, skin side down, on paper towel and refrigerating overnight.

The next day, dry-fry the sichuan peppercorns and salt in a frying pan for 3 minutes over medium heat, stirring constantly, until the salt turns golden. Using a mortar and pestle, pound until very fine, then set aside.

To make the Asian greens, wash the Chinese broccoli well, taking care to remove all the dirt. Discard any large or old leaves and thinly slice the stems on an angle. Heat a splash of oil in a wok over high heat and cook the garlic and ginger for 2–3 minutes, stirring often and making sure the garlic doesn't burn. Add the Chinese broccoli and broccolini and toss for 1–2 minutes before adding the stock. Cover with a lid and cook for 3–4 minutes, tossing occasionally to ensure the greens cook evenly. Remove the lid and season with soy sauce.

Remove the quail from the refrigerator and make sure the skin is as dry as possible, otherwise they will spatter when fried. Heat 4 cm (1½ in) of oil in a wok or deep saucepan; the oil is hot enough for frying when a cube of bread turns brown in 20 seconds. Fry 2–3 quail at a time until crispy, then drain on paper towel.

Arrange the quail on a serving platter and sprinkle with the salt and pepper mix. Serve with lime wedges, the Asian greens and an additional bowl of salt and pepper mix, if desired.

# Pomegranate

## Pomegranate chicken with cherry tomato salad

SERVES
·
4

Marinate four 125 g (4½ oz) boneless, skinless chicken breasts for up to 4 hours in a mixture of 2 tablespoons lemon juice, 2 tablespoons pomegranate molasses, 2 tablespoons olive oil, salt and freshly ground black pepper. Meanwhile, to make the cherry tomato salad, take 500 g (1 lb 2 oz) mixed cherry tomatoes (a mix of regular, yellow pear, baby roma and heirloom varieties is lovely). Halve the tomatoes and put in a bowl along with the seeds from ½ pomegranate, 1 tablespoon lemon juice, 2 tablespoons pomegranate molasses, 1 handful each of chopped flat-leaf (Italian) parsley, coriander (cilantro) leaves and mint, and 80 ml (2½ fl oz/⅓ cup) olive oil. Season well with salt and freshly ground black pepper. Once marinated, cook the chicken on a barbecue or in a heavy-based frying pan for 6–8 minutes on each side over medium heat, until cooked through. Rest for 5 minutes before slicing and serving with the cherry tomato salad.

## Haloumi with za'atar and pomegranate

SERVES
·
4 AS A
STARTER

Heat a splash of olive oil in a large frying pan over medium–high heat. Cut 300 g (10½ oz) haloumi into 5 mm (¼ in) slices, add to the hot pan and cook for 2–3 minutes on each side, until golden brown. Remove and place on a serving platter. Sprinkle 1 teaspoon za'atar and 1 small handful of torn mint over the top. Season the haloumi with freshly ground black pepper and drizzle 1 tablespoon pomegranate molasses and the juice of half a lemon over the top. Scatter pomegranate seeds over the top if desired.

## Pomegranate fattoush

SERVES
·
4–6

Soak ½ thinly sliced red onion in hot water for 2 minutes. Drain and cool before tossing with 1 teaspoon sumac. Cut 125 g (4½ oz) pide (Turkish bread) into 1 cm (½ in) cubes. Heat a generous splash of oil in a heavy-based frying pan over medium heat. Cook the bread cubes for 6–8 minutes, stirring often, until golden brown all over. Toss the bread with the onion, 1 chopped baby cos (romaine) lettuce, 1 sliced Lebanese (short) cucumber and 1 handful of flat-leaf (Italian) parsley leaves. Combine 2 tablespoons lemon juice, 1 tablespoon pomegranate molasses, salt and freshly ground black pepper, then whisk in 3 tablespoons extra-virgin olive oil. Dress the salad just before serving and garnish with pomegranate seeds.

# Five-spiced duck and pomegranate salad

Pomegranate is such a beautiful fruit. It is very commonly used in savoury dishes, where it adds a lovely texture and deliciously fresh burst of flavour. **SERVES • 4**

2 × 200 G (7 OZ) DUCK BREASTS, SKIN ON

1 TEASPOON CHINESE FIVE-SPICE

½ TEASPOON CHILLI FLAKES

1 TEASPOON SEA SALT

2 TABLESPOONS OIL

SEEDS FROM 1 POMEGRANATE

1 BABY COS (ROMAINE) LETTUCE, LEAVES PICKED

100 G (3½ OZ) WATERCRESS

100 G (3½ OZ) BEAN SPROUTS, SOAKED IN COLD WATER AND DRAINED

3 SPRING ONIONS (SCALLIONS), THINLY SLICED

30 G (1 OZ/1 CUP) CORIANDER (CILANTRO) LEAVES

10 G (¼ OZ/½ CUP) VIETNAMESE MINT OR MINT

80 G (2¾ OZ/½ CUP) ROASTED PEANUTS

50 G (1¾ OZ) VERMICELLI NOODLES, BLANCHED

2 TABLESPOONS LIME JUICE

2 TEASPOONS SESAME OIL

SALT AND FRESHLY GROUND BLACK PEPPER

Preheat the oven to 180°C (350°F).

Score the skin of the duck breasts using a small, sharp knife. Mix together the Chinese five-spice and chilli flakes with the 1 teaspoon of salt, and sprinkle over the duck skin.

Heat a large heavy-based ovenproof frying pan over medium–high heat. Add the oil and fry the duck for 3–4 minutes on each side until golden brown. Transfer to the oven and cook for 5 minutes, or until medium-rare. Cover and rest for 5 minutes.

In a large bowl, combine the pomegranate seeds, lettuce, watercress, bean sprouts, spring onion, coriander, mint, peanuts and noodles. Dress with the lime juice and sesame oil and season with salt and freshly ground black pepper.

Slice the duck thinly and toss with the salad. Divide among four plates and serve immediately.

# Fig

## Zabaglione and figs

SERVES
•
4

In a large stainless-steel bowl, lightly whisk together 6 egg yolks and 115 g (4 oz/½ cup) caster (superfine) sugar. Stir in 2 tablespoons Marsala and place the bowl over a saucepan of simmering water. Whisk continuously for 5 minutes, or until the mixture thickens and doubles in size. Remove from the heat and continue to whisk until the zabaglione cools. Spoon into four serving glasses, cover and refrigerate for 3–4 hours, until cool. To serve, cut 2–4 figs into slices and arrange on top of the zabaglione.

## Ricotta-stuffed figs

SERVES
•
4

In a bowl, mix together the zest of 1 orange, 3 tablespoons chopped pistachios, 2 tablespoons caster (superfine) sugar and 250 g (9 oz/1 cup) ricotta. Take 12 figs and split them crossways to open them up. Add a spoonful of the ricotta mix to the centre of each fig and gently pinch the figs slightly closed. Place on a baking tray, drizzle with honey and cook in a preheated 180°C (350°F) oven for 10 minutes, or until the figs are hot. Serve with mascarpone.

## Fig clafoutis

SERVES
•
4

Preheat the oven to 180°C (350°F) and lightly butter an ovenproof dish. Beat 3 eggs in a bowl along with 80 g (2¾ oz/⅓ cup) caster (superfine) sugar, 250 g (9 oz/1 cup) plain yoghurt, 250 ml (8½ fl oz/1 cup) milk, 2 tablespoons self-raising flour and 1 teaspoon natural vanilla extract. Halve 6 figs and arrange in the base of the prepared dish. Pour the batter over the figs and bake for 45 minutes. When ready, the clafoutis will be puffed and golden.

# Chestnut risotto with sage and pancetta

Buy a good-quality pancetta from your local deli and ask them to cut slices approximately 1 centimetre (½ inch) thick. Then cut into large dice to add good-sized pieces to your dish. Fully develop the flavour of the pancetta by cooking it until it's golden brown. SERVES • 4–6

375 G (13 OZ) LARGE CHESTNUTS

OIL, FOR COOKING

100 G (3½ OZ) PANCETTA, DICED

1 ONION, DICED

1 GARLIC CLOVE, CRUSHED

1 LEEK, WHITE PART ONLY, THINLY SLICED (OPTIONAL)

1 CARROT, FINELY DICED (OPTIONAL)

300 G (10½ OZ) RISOTTO RICE

125 ML (4 FL OZ/½ CUP) WHITE WINE

750 ML–1 LITRE (25½–34 FL OZ/3–4 CUPS) HOT VEGETABLE OR CHICKEN STOCK

40 G (1½ OZ) PARMIGIANO REGGIANO, GRATED

50 G (1¾ OZ) BUTTER, DICED

2 TABLESPOONS CHOPPED SAGE

Preheat the oven to 180°C (350°F).

Bring a saucepan of water to the boil. Meanwhile, cut a slit in the bottom of each chestnut. Add the chestnuts to the boiling water, cover and reduce to a simmer. Cook for 15–20 minutes, or until tender. Remove from the heat and while still warm (it's easier), peel the hard shell and the inner skin from each chestnut. Roughly chop the cooked chestnuts. Set aside.

Heat a large heavy-based saucepan over medium heat. Add the oil and the pancetta and cook for 5–6 minutes or until golden brown. Remove the pancetta from the heat and set aside.

Wipe the pan clean of any fat and return to the heat. Add 2 tablespoons of oil, the onion, garlic, leek and carrot (if using) and cook for 3–4 minutes until fragrant and soft. Add the rice and stir to coat it with the oil, then cook briefly. Add the wine and stir until it is absorbed. Return the pancetta to the pan.

Begin adding the hot stock: just enough to cover the rice at first, adding a ladleful at a time as the stock is absorbed. Stir well with each addition. Continue cooking for 15–20 minutes, until the rice is just done but each grain is still slightly firm in the centre.

Remove from the heat. Add the chestnuts, cheese, butter and sage, and stir until the risotto is creamy and the cheese has melted. Check the seasoning and serve.

# Eggplant (aubergine)

## Eggplant rolls with olive tapenade

MAKES
•
16

Cut 2 eggplants (aubergines) lengthways into thin slices and sprinkle with salt; allow to drain in a colander for 30 minutes. Rinse and dry well. Pan-fry the eggplant slices in olive oil until golden brown on both sides. Drain and allow to cool. Make tapenade by mixing together 100 g (3½ oz) chopped pitted kalamata olives, 2 tablespoons chopped flat-leaf (Italian) parsley, 1 finely chopped anchovy fillet and 1 tablespoon chopped capers, adding enough olive oil to make a paste. Lay the eggplant slices out flat, add some chopped basil and crumbled feta and roll up. Spoon the tapenade over the top and serve.

## Eggplant with tomato, mint and chilli

SERVES
•
6 AS A
SIDE DISH

Dice 2 eggplants (aubergines) into 2 cm (¾ in) chunks and sprinkle with salt; allow to drain in a colander for 30 minutes. Rinse and dry well. Place a large heavy-based frying pan over medium heat and add enough oil to cover the base of the pan. Cook the eggplant in batches until golden brown, adding more oil if necessary. Remove the eggplant from the pan then add 2 thinly sliced red chillies and 4 diced tomatoes, with a splash more oil if necessary. Cook briefly until the tomatoes just start to collapse then remove from the pan. Add to the eggplant and allow to cool slightly. Add the juice from 1 lemon and 2 tablespoons chopped mint, and season to taste with salt and freshly ground black pepper. Serve at room temperature. This is a perfect side dish for roast chicken or barbecued lamb.

## Pomegranate baba ghanoush

SERVES
•
4–6

Burn 2 eggplants (aubergines) over a barbecue or hot coals, or over a gas stovetop, rotating as each side burns. Depending on the size of the eggplants, you may need to finish them in the oven to ensure they are cooked through. Remove and discard the burnt skin from the eggplants and roughly mash the flesh. Add 2 tablespoons tahini, 125 g (4½ oz/½ cup) plain yoghurt, 2 tablespoons pomegranate molasses, 3–4 tablespoons extra-virgin olive oil, salt and freshly ground black pepper. Stir well to combine. Spoon into a bowl, top with the seeds from ½ pomegranate and drizzle with extra-virgin olive oil. Serve with toasted pitta (Lebanese bread).

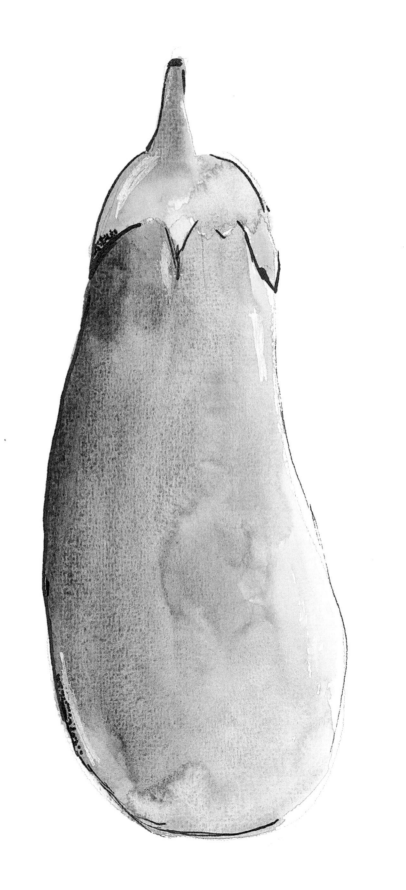

# Slow-roasted lamb with pomegranate and sumac glaze

Try this meltingly tender lamb, which pulls apart with a couple of forks, for a late Sunday lunch. The pomegranate molasses cuts through the fattiness of the lamb and adds a sweet–savoury glaze when combined with that essential Middle Eastern spice, sumac. SERVES • 6

2 TABLESPOONS POMEGRANATE MOLASSES

2 TABLESPOONS OLIVE OIL

2 GARLIC CLOVES, CRUSHED

2 TABLESPOONS SUMAC

SALT AND FRESHLY GROUND BLACK PEPPER

2 KG (4 LB 6 OZ) LAMB SHOULDER OR LEG, BONE-IN

125 ML (4 FL OZ/½ CUP) CHICKEN STOCK OR WATER

Preheat the oven to 140°C (275°F).

To prepare the glaze, combine the pomegranate molasses, olive oil, garlic, sumac, salt and freshly ground black pepper together, mixing into a paste.

Lightly score the skin of the meat, making shallow incisions through any fat. Spread the glaze over the lamb, and into the scoring. Place the lamb in a roasting tin, cover with foil and roast for 5 hours, turning occasionally. Make sure to seal the foil securely each time.

After 5 hours, remove the foil and add the chicken stock or water to the tin. Return to the oven for a further hour, turning the lamb two or three times. Ensure the lamb is cooked until it is literally falling apart. Transfer the lamb to a large serving platter and cover with foil.

Pour any excess oil from the roasting tin and place the tin over medium heat. Bring the liquid almost to the boil, using a wooden spoon to scrape the bottom of the tin.

Check the seasoning and adjust if necessary. Pour the pan juices over the lamb to serve.

# Beef braise with mushrooms

Rich with red wine and herbs, this hearty braise is just the thing for colder days when the nights are drawing in. A full-bodied wine will help give it that extra depth of flavour.
SERVES • 4

OLIVE OIL, FOR FRYING

1 KG (2 LB 3 OZ) BRAISING BEEF, SUCH AS BLADE, DICED

1 ONION, DICED

2 CARROTS, DICED

125 ML (4 FL OZ/½ CUP) RED WINE

375 ML (12½ FL OZ/1½ CUPS) BEEF STOCK, PLUS EXTRA IF NECESSARY

250 ML (8½ FL OZ/1 CUP) TOMATO SUGO

2 BAY LEAVES

2–3 THYME SPRIGS

250 G (9 OZ) SWISS BROWN MUSHROOMS, CHOPPED

2 TABLESPOONS CHOPPED FLAT-LEAF (ITALIAN) PARSLEY

CREAMY POLENTA OR MASHED POTATO, TO SERVE

Preheat the oven to 180°C (350°F).

Heat a large flameproof casserole dish over medium–high heat, add a splash of olive oil and cook the beef in batches until golden brown all over. Remove and set aside.

Add another splash of oil to the dish and cook the onion for 2–3 minutes, until soft. Add the carrot and cook for a few minutes before returning the beef to the dish.

Add the red wine and allow to reduce by half. Add the beef stock and tomato sugo, along with the bay leaves and thyme, and season well with salt and freshly ground black pepper. Bring to the boil, then reduce to a simmer. Cover and cook in the oven for 1 hour.

Remove from the oven, gently stir in the mushrooms, more stock if needed, and return to the oven for a further 1 hour.

When the beef is tender, check for seasoning and finish with the parsley. Serve with creamy polenta or mashed potato.

# Orange

## Turkey breast with chestnut and orange stuffing

Preheat the oven to 160°C (320°F). Soak 60 g (2 oz/¾ cup) fresh breadcrumbs in 125 ml (4 fl oz/½ cup) orange juice for 10 minutes. Heat 2 tablespoons olive oil in a saucepan over medium heat and cook 1 diced onion and 2 crushed garlic cloves until soft. Add to the breadcrumb mixture and mix in 200 g (7 oz) peeled, roasted chestnuts, the zest of 1 orange, 2 tablespoons chopped flat-leaf (Italian) parsley, 1 egg, salt and freshly ground black pepper, until well combined. Place a 1 kg (2 lb 3 oz) turkey breast, skin side down, on a clean work surface. Push the tenderloin to one side and spoon the stuffing down the centre. Roll the turkey around the stuffing so it sits skin side up; secure it with kitchen string at 2 cm (¾ in) intervals. Oil the turkey breast and season well. Put it in a roasting tin and bake for 1 hour and 20 minutes, or until a meat thermometer reads 77–80°C (170–176°F). Transfer to a dish, cover with foil and rest for 10–15 minutes before serving.

## Quinoa and orange salad

Bring 200 g (7 oz/1 cup) quinoa and 500 ml (17 fl oz/2 cups) vegetable stock or salted water to the boil in a saucepan. Cover and simmer over low heat for 15 minutes, or until all the liquid is absorbed. Remove from the heat and allow to rest, covered, for 5 minutes. Transfer the quinoa to a bowl and fluff with a fork as it cools. Cut the peel from 2 oranges and slice the flesh into segments, reserving any juice. Combine the orange segments with the quinoa, 70 g (2½ oz/ ½ cup) roasted, shelled pepitas (pumpkin seeds), 50 g (1¾ oz/⅓ cup) toasted almonds, 50 g (1¾ oz/⅓ cup) toasted pistachios, 2 thinly sliced spring onions (scallions), 2 tablespoons chopped mint and 1 handful of flat-leaf (Italian) parsley. Season well with salt and freshly ground black pepper. Add the reserved orange juice and 2–3 tablespoons extra-virgin olive oil. Toss to combine.

# Yoghurt panna cotta with caramelised peaches and salted praline

An elegant twist on the traditional panna cotta, this dessert elevates the wonderfully fragrant flesh of in-season peaches by caramelising them under a hot grill. SERVES • 6

2 × 5 G (¼ OZ) GELATINE LEAVES

250 ML (8½ FL OZ/1 CUP) CREAM

80 G (2¾ OZ/⅓ CUP) CASTER (SUPERFINE) SUGAR

1 TEASPOON NATURAL VANILLA EXTRACT

375 G (13 OZ/1½ CUPS) PLAIN YOGHURT

**SALTED PRALINE**

80 G (2¾ OZ/⅓ CUP) CASTER (SUPERFINE) SUGAR

½ TEASPOON SALT

80 G (2¾ OZ/½ CUP) BLANCHED ALMONDS, TOASTED

**CARAMELISED PEACHES**

6 PEACHES

ICING (CONFECTIONERS') SUGAR, FOR SPRINKLING

To make the salted praline, put the caster sugar and 2 tablespoons water in a small saucepan. Heat gently to dissolve the sugar, then bring to the boil. Swirl the liquid over the heat (do not stir) to prevent sugar crystals forming, and cook to a light brown colour. Remove from the heat and stir in the salt and toasted almonds. Pour onto a lightly oiled baking tray and leave until set hard. When completely cold, remove from the tray and chop into bite-sized pieces.

Soak the gelatine leaves in cold water for 5 minutes, or until softened. Remove from the water and squeeze gently to remove excess liquid before using.

Meanwhile, in a saucepan, bring the cream, caster sugar and vanilla to the boil. Remove from the heat and briefly allow to cool before adding the gelatine and stirring until dissolved. Strain the liquid through a sieve, whisk in the yoghurt and then pour into six 125 ml (4 fl oz/½ cup) dariole moulds. Refrigerate until set, at least 4 hours or overnight.

Once the panna cottas have set, preheat the grill (broiler) to hot. Cut the peaches in half and remove the stones. Sprinkle the cut sides lightly with icing sugar. Cook under the grill for 5–10 minutes, or until the peaches just begin to brown.

Meanwhile, remove the panna cottas from the refrigerator and, using a small spatula or knife, work the puddings away from the edge of the moulds. Stand the moulds in boiling water for 4–5 seconds, place a plate on top of each one, then carefully invert so the plate is on the bottom. Gently shake to dislodge the panna cottas.

Cut the peach halves into wedges and serve alongside the panna cotta, sprinkling the chopped praline over the top to finish.

# Cranberry

## Almond and cranberry stuffing

Heat 2 tablespoons oil in a saucepan over medium heat. Add 1 finely diced onion and cook for 5–6 minutes, until soft. Add 2 crushed garlic cloves, cook briefly then remove from the heat to cool slightly. Put the onion and garlic in a bowl along with 2 tablespoons chopped flat-leaf (Italian) parsley, 100 g (3½ oz) dried cranberries, 80 g (2¾ oz/½ cup) toasted almonds, 240 g (8½ oz/3 cups) fresh breadcrumbs and 1 lightly beaten egg. Season well with salt and freshly ground black pepper and mix well to combine. Use the stuffing to stuff a whole chicken or turkey, or spoon into a loaf (bar) tin lined with baking paper and cook alongside your roast for 30 minutes, or until crunchy on top.

## Maple and cranberry chicken drumsticks

Combine 2 tablespoons cranberry sauce or relish, 2 tablespoons maple syrup, 2 tablespoons olive oil, salt and freshly ground black pepper. Pour the mixture over 1 kg (2 lb 3 oz) chicken drumsticks or, if preferred, chicken drumettes, wings or ribs. Allow to marinate for at least 1 hour. Preheat the oven to 180°C (350°F). Line a deep baking tray with baking paper and arrange the chicken pieces in a single layer. Cook for 1 hour, turning often, until the chicken is golden brown and cooked through. Serve with mashed potatoes and steamed green beans.

# Honey-roasted nectarines with orange-blossom labne

Roasting nectarines like this intensifies their flavour and delivers a whole new level of caramelised sweetness, making them the perfect accompaniment for this bright, fresh cheese. SERVES • 4–6

500 G (1 LB 2 OZ/2 CUPS) GREEK-STYLE YOGHURT

1–2 TABLESPOONS ORANGE-BLOSSOM WATER

4–6 NECTARINES, HALVED AND STONES REMOVED

1 TABLESPOON BUTTER

3 TABLESPOONS HONEY

1 PINCH GROUND CARDAMOM

To make the labne, line a sieve with muslin (cheesecloth). Add the yoghurt, set the sieve over a bowl, and refrigerate overnight.

Discard the whey that has dripped into the bowl below the sieve, and transfer the labne to a bowl. Stir in the orange-blossom water and set aside.

Preheat the oven to 180°C (350°F).

Arrange the nectarines snugly in a small baking dish.

In a saucepan over low heat, melt the butter together with the honey and stir in the ground cardamom. Drizzle the butter mixture over the nectarines.

Bake the nectarines for 15–20 minutes, until tender and lightly browned. Serve hot, with a generous spoonful of labne.

# Classic raspberry sponge cake

There's something undeniably nostalgic about a good sponge cake filled with a little whipped cream and a layer of raspberry jam. Topped with fresh raspberries, it looks a picture, too. Maybe it's time to revive the tradition of afternoon tea just so we can enjoy a treat such as this. SERVES • 6–8

4 EGGS

115 G (4 OZ/½ CUP) CASTER (SUPERFINE) SUGAR

100 G (3½ OZ/⅔ CUP) PLAIN (ALL-PURPOSE) FLOUR, PLUS EXTRA FOR SPRINKLING

RASPBERRY JAM, FOR SPREADING

250 ML (8½ FL OZ/1 CUP) CREAM, WHIPPED

150 G (5½ OZ) RASPBERRIES

ICING (CONFECTIONERS') SUGAR, TO SERVE

Preheat the oven to 180°C (350°F).

Grease a 20 cm (8 in) springform cake tin and line the base and side with baking paper. Butter the paper and sprinkle it with a little flour to ensure that the batter doesn't stick.

Beat the eggs and caster sugar together for 8–10 minutes, until thick, pale and at least doubled in volume.

Sift in the flour and fold gently, then spoon the mix into the prepared cake tin. Bake in the oven for 15–20 minutes, until a skewer inserted into the centre of the cake comes out clean.

Allow the cake to cool on a wire rack. When cool, remove the cake from the tin and peel away the baking paper. When completely cold, cut the sponge in half horizontally and spread a layer of jam, then whipped cream, on the bottom half of the cake. Replace the top of the sponge, arrange the raspberries on top and dust with icing sugar.

# Tangelo

## Tangelo syrup cake

SERVES
·
8

Beat 250 g (9 oz) softened diced butter, the zest of 2 tangelos and 230 g (8 oz/ 1 cup) caster (superfine) sugar until light and fluffy. Add 3 egg yolks and stir until combined. Fold in 150 g (5½ oz/1 cup) self-raising flour, 185 g (6½ oz/1½ cups) fine semolina and 250 ml (8½ fl oz/1 cup) buttermilk. Beat 3 egg whites until stiff and fold through the cake batter. Spoon into a greased 23 cm (9 in) springform cake tin. Bake in a preheated 180°C (350°F) oven for 30–40 minutes, or until a skewer inserted into the centre of the cake comes out clean. Remove from the oven and allow to cool. Meanwhile, prepare a syrup by putting the juice from 2 tangelos and 170 g (6 oz/¾ cup) caster (superfine) sugar in a saucepan and cooking over a low heat until the sugar dissolves. Set aside to cool slightly. To serve, remove the cake from the tin and pour the syrup over the top. Serve while warm with cream.

## Tangelo and almond cake

SERVES
·
6–8

Preheat the oven to 180°C (350°F) and grease a 23 cm (9 in) round cake tin. Put 2 tangelos in a saucepan, cover with water and bring to the boil over high heat. Reduce to a simmer and cook for 30–40 minutes, until the fruit is soft. Allow to cool. Drain, purée the fruit, and strain through a fine-mesh sieve. Beat 5 eggs and 230 g (8 oz/1 cup) caster (superfine) sugar until the mixture is pale and has doubled in volume, about 5 minutes. Mix together 250 g (9 oz/2½ cups) ground almonds and 1 teaspoon baking powder. Add the tangelo purée and almond mixture to the beaten eggs, and beat to incorporate completely. Pour into the prepared cake tin and bake for about 1 hour, or until light brown and firm in the centre.

# Banana

## Banoffee pie

SERVES
•
8

Make dulce de leche by simmering a tin of unopened condensed milk in a saucepan of water, ensuring the tin stays covered with water at all times, for 2½ hours. Remove from the water and allow to cool at room temperature before opening. Meanwhile, put 100 g (3½ oz) plain sweet biscuits (cookies) and 50 g (1¾ oz) pretzels in a food processor and whiz to form fine crumbs. Add 60 g (2 oz) melted butter and process briefly. Press the biscuit mix into the base of a 20 cm (8 in) springform cake tin and put in the refrigerator to set for at least 20 minutes. To serve, spread the tin of dulce de leche over the top of the biscuit base, top with banana slices and then add enough whipped cream to cover. Grate some dark chocolate over the cream and serve immediately.

## Caramel and banana cake

SERVES
•
6–8

Cream 220 g (8 oz) softened diced butter and 230 g (8 oz/1 cup firmly packed) soft brown sugar until pale and fluffy. Beat in 3 tablespoons golden syrup or dark corn syrup and 1 teaspoon natural vanilla extract. Add 3 eggs, one at a time, fully incorporating after each addition. Add 400 g (14 oz/2⅔ cups) self-raising flour and 170 ml (5½ fl oz/⅔ cup) milk and mix until well combined. Spoon into a lined 23 cm (9 in) springform cake tin and bake in a preheated 180°C (350°F) oven for 40 minutes, or until a skewer inserted into the centre of the cake comes out clean. Meanwhile, to make caramel icing, put 115 g (4 oz/½ cup) soft brown sugar, 2 tablespoons butter and 2 tablespoons golden syrup or dark corn syrup in a saucepan and melt. Remove, cool slightly and then add 125 g (4½ oz/1 cup) icing (confectioners') sugar, whisking until combined. Allow the cake to cool before topping it with the caramel icing.

## Banana and dulce de leche sundaes

SERVES
•
4

Make dulce de leche by simmering a tin of unopened condensed milk in a saucepan of water, ensuring the tin stays covered with water at all times, for 2½ hours. Remove from the water and allow to cool at room temperature before opening. Meanwhile, make hazelnut praline by placing 115 g (4 oz/½ cup) caster (superfine) sugar in a saucepan with 2 tablespoons water. Allow to come to the boil, ensuring the sugar has dissolved. Cook for 5 minutes, or until the sugar starts to caramelise. Add a handful of roasted, skinned hazelnuts, swirl to coat, then pour onto a lined baking tray and allow to cool. Once the praline is cool and hard, chop roughly. Take four sundae glasses and put a spoonful of good-quality vanilla ice cream in each. Using 4 bananas, add slices of ½ banana to each glass and top with a spoonful of dulce de leche (you may need to warm it slightly so you can drizzle it) and a scattering of praline. Repeat with another scoop of ice cream and the remaining banana, and finish with dulce de leche and more hazelnut praline.

# Cauliflower

## Cauliflower and coriander fritters

MAKES
•
15

Preheat the oven to 180°C (350°F). Cut ½ cauliflower into small florets and blanch in boiling water for 1–2 minutes. Drain and set aside to cool. Mix together 150 g (5½ oz/1 cup) self-raising flour, 1 pinch of salt, freshly ground black pepper, 1 teaspoon ground cumin, 2 teaspoons ground coriander, 4 eggs, 2 tablespoons chopped coriander (cilantro) leaves and 2 tablespoons plain yoghurt until smooth. Add the cauliflower. Heat a splash of oil in a heavy-based frying pan over medium–high heat, add spoonfuls of the batter and cook for 3–4 minutes on each side until golden. Put the cooked fritters in the oven on a baking tray to keep warm while cooking the remaining batter. Meanwhile, to make lime yoghurt dipping sauce, mix 125 g (4½ oz/½ cup) plain yoghurt with the zest and juice of 1 lime, and 1 tablespoon extra-virgin olive oil. Season well with salt and freshly ground black pepper. Serve the warm fritters with the dipping sauce.

## Spiced cauliflower

SERVES
•
4 AS A
SIDE DISH

Soak 1 tablespoon tamarind pulp in 125 ml (4 fl oz/½ cup) boiling water for 5–10 minutes. Use your fingers to work the pulp free from the tamarind seeds. Strain the tamarind, reserving the liquid. Heat 1–2 tablespoons ghee or coconut oil in a heavy-based frying pan over medium–high heat. Fry 2 teaspoons chilli powder, 2 teaspoons ground cumin, 2 teaspoons ground coriander and 1 teaspoon turmeric, stirring often, until fragrant. Cut ½ cauliflower into small florets and add to the hot spice mix along with the tamarind liquid. Season well with salt and freshly ground black pepper. Bring to the boil, then reduce the heat and cook for 5–6 minutes, stirring often, until the cauliflower is just cooked. Scatter coriander (cilantro) leaves over the top and serve alongside your favourite curry.

## Lentil and cauliflower curry

SERVES
•
4

Heat a large saucepan over medium–high heat. Add a splash of oil and 1 diced onion and cook for 5–6 minutes, or until the onion is soft. Add 2 crushed garlic cloves, 2 teaspoons grated ginger and 2 tablespoons curry paste and cook for 1–2 minutes. Add 250 ml (8½ fl oz/1 cup) tomato passata (puréed tomatoes), 250 ml (8½ fl oz/1 cup) vegetable stock and ½ cauliflower, roughly chopped, and bring to the boil. Season with salt. Reduce the heat and simmer for 10–15 minutes. Add 400 g (14 oz) tinned lentils (drained and rinsed) and 100 g (3½ oz) baby English spinach leaves and cook for 1–2 minutes. Check the seasoning. Add a handful of coriander (cilantro) leaves and serve with steamed rice.

# Barbecued quail with baby carrot salad and black quinoa

This mouthwatering combination of delicate charred quail, soft roasted roots and crunchy grains and seeds will have you firing up the barbecue on the coldest of winter's days. SERVES • 6

ZEST OF 2 LEMONS

6 THYME SPRIGS, LEAVES PICKED

3 GARLIC CLOVES, FINELY CHOPPED

80 ML (2½ FL OZ/⅓ CUP) EXTRA-VIRGIN OLIVE OIL

SALT AND FRESHLY GROUND BLACK PEPPER

6 LARGE QUAILS, SPATCHCOCKED (ASK YOUR BUTCHER TO DO THIS)

100 G (3½ OZ/½ CUP) BLACK QUINOA

70 G (2½ OZ/½ CUP) PEPITAS (PUMPKIN SEEDS)

50 G (1¾ OZ/⅓ CUP) ALMONDS

50 G (1¾ OZ/⅓) PISTACHIO NUTS

2 ORANGES

2 SPRING ONIONS (SCALLIONS), THINLY SLICED

2 TABLESPOONS CHOPPED MINT

1 HANDFUL OF FLAT-LEAF (ITALIAN) PARSLEY

## BABY CARROT SALAD

500 G (1 LB 2 OZ) BABY CARROTS, SCRUBBED AND PEELED IF NECESSARY

EXTRA-VIRGIN OLIVE OIL

2 TABLESPOONS FENNEL SEEDS, TOASTED IN A DRY FRYING PAN UNTIL FRAGRANT

2 TABLESPOONS LEMON JUICE

SALT AND FRESHLY GROUND BLACK PEPPER

2 PRESERVED LEMON QUARTERS, PITH DISCARDED AND SKIN THINLY SLICED

30 G (1 OZ/1 CUP) CORIANDER (CILANTRO) LEAVES

10 G (¼ OZ/½ CUP) MINT, TORN IN HALF IF LARGE

In a small bowl, mix together the lemon zest, thyme, garlic, 2 tablespoons of the extra-virgin olive oil, salt and freshly ground black pepper. Pour the mixture over the quails and refrigerate for up to 4 hours.

Cook the quinoa in a saucepan of boiling salted water, stirring often, for about 12 minutes, or until tender. Drain and allow to cool.

To make the carrot salad, preheat the oven to 180°C (350°F). Place the carrots in a single layer on a lined baking tray. Drizzle with extra-virgin olive oil, scatter with the toasted fennel seeds and season well with salt and freshly ground black pepper. Roast for 15–20 minutes, or until the carrots are just cooked. Remove and set aside to cool slightly. Just before serving, toss 1 tablespoon of extra-virgin olive oil, the lemon juice, preserved lemon, coriander and mint through the carrots.

Meanwhile, in a dry frying pan over a low–medium heat, toast the pepitas, almonds and pistachios separately until golden brown and fragrant, taking care not to burn them.

Cut the peel and bitter white pith off the oranges with a sharp knife and cut between the membranes to remove each orange segment, catching any juice over a bowl. Put the segments in a separate bowl along with the quinoa, pepitas, almonds, pistachios, spring onion, mint and parsley. Season well. Add the reserved orange juice and the remaining extra-virgin olive oil and mix well.

Heat a barbecue grill until hot. Place the quails on the barbecue, skin side down, and cook for 5–6 minutes. Turn the quails over, and cook for a further 4–5 minutes. Remove from the heat, cover and allow to rest in a warm place for 5 minutes. Serve hot, with the warm carrot salad and quinoa.

# Broccoli

## Pasta with bacon and broccoli

SERVES
·
4

Bring a large saucepan of salted water to the boil over high heat. Add 400 g (14 oz) pasta and stir until the water returns to the boil. Reduce the heat, cover and cook the pasta for 8 minutes. Heat a frying pan over medium–high heat. Add a splash of oil and 1 diced onion and cook for 3–4 minutes. Add 200 g (7 oz) diced bacon and cook for 3–4 minutes, until it starts to turn golden brown. Add 3 tablespoons stock and bring to the boil. Add the chopped florets from a head of broccoli and cook for 1–2 minutes. Season with salt and freshly ground black pepper and add 2 tablespoons chopped flat-leaf (Italian) parsley. Drain the pasta and toss with the bacon and broccoli, along with a handful of grated parmesan.

## Thai chicken and broccoli stir-fry

SERVES
·
4

Bring 3 tablespoons coconut cream to the boil in a saucepan and add 1 tablespoon Thai red curry paste. Allow the paste to cook in the natural oils of the coconut cream for 4–5 minutes, stirring often. Add 2 teaspoons fish sauce, 2 teaspoons grated palm sugar (jaggery) and 125 ml (4 fl oz/½ cup) coconut milk and leave the sauce to simmer. Heat a wok until hot. Add 1 tablespoon oil and 4 sliced spring onions (scallions), cooking briefly before adding 2 thinly sliced boneless, skinless chicken breasts. Cook until brown all over. Remove the chicken and add to the curry sauce, along with 1 thinly sliced carrot and 1 head of broccoli cut into small florets. Allow to cook for 5–6 minutes, stirring often. Check the seasoning, adding more fish sauce if needed. Finish with 2 tablespoons chopped coriander (cilantro) leaves and serve with steamed rice.

# Salmon with broccoli and anchovy sauce

Anchovies bring a lovely salty hit to any dish. They are a particularly good complement to rich fish such as salmon. **SERVES • 6**

1 HANDFUL OF FLAT-LEAF (ITALIAN) PARSLEY LEAVES

1 SMALL ROSEMARY SPRIG, LEAVES PICKED

10 ANCHOVY FILLETS

80 ML (2½ FL OZ/⅓ CUP) EXTRA-VIRGIN OLIVE OIL

ZEST AND JUICE OF 1 LEMON

FRESHLY GROUND BLACK PEPPER

2 TABLESPOONS OLIVE OIL

6 × 180 G (6½ OZ) SALMON FILLETS, SKIN ON

500 G (1 LB 2 OZ) BROCCOLI, CUT INTO FLORETS

Preheat the oven to 180°C (350°F).

Grind the parsley and rosemary to a paste using a mortar and pestle. Add the anchovies and pound lightly. Stir in the extra-virgin olive oil, and lemon zest and juice. Season with freshly ground black pepper.

Heat the olive oil in a large heavy-based ovenproof frying pan over medium–high heat. Add the salmon, flesh side down, and cook for 3–4 minutes. Turn over and cook for a further 2–3 minutes. Transfer to the oven and cook for 3–4 minutes, or until the salmon is medium-rare.

Meanwhile, boil the broccoli for 2–3 minutes, drain and toss with 1–2 tablespoons of the anchovy sauce.

Divide the salmon and broccoli among plates and drizzle with the remaining sauce. Serve immediately.

# Parsnip

## Roast parsnip two ways

SERVES
•
4 AS A
SIDE DISH

Preheat the oven to 180°C (350°F). Peel 6 parsnips, cut in half lengthways, place on a lined baking tray and drizzle with olive oil. Either sprinkle with 2 teaspoons ground cumin and 2–3 thyme sprigs, or drizzle with Worcestershire sauce and 1 tablespoon honey. Season well with salt and freshly ground black pepper and toss to combine. Roast for 40–45 minutes, until crisp and golden.

## Shepherd's pie with spiced parsnip mash

SERVES
•
4

Preheat the oven to 180°C (350°F). Heat a splash of oil in a large heavy-based saucepan over medium–high heat. Sauté 1 diced onion, 1 diced carrot and 2 diced celery stalks for 5–6 minutes, stirring often. Add 500 g (1 lb 2 oz) minced (ground) lamb and cook, stirring often, for a further 5–6 minutes, until browned. Add ½ teaspoon ground cumin, a splash of Worcestershire sauce, 400 g (14 oz) tinned chopped tomatoes and enough beef stock to cover, around 250 ml (8½ fl oz/1 cup). Bring to the boil and season with salt and freshly ground black pepper. Simmer for 30 minutes, stirring often. Meanwhile, to make the spiced parsnip mash, peel and cut 1 kg (2 lb 3 oz) parsnips into even-sized pieces. Boil until tender. Drain. Mash with ½ teaspoon ground cumin, 50 g (1¾ oz) butter, salt and freshly ground black pepper. Once cooked, spoon the lamb mixture into a deep casserole dish. Cover with the spiced parsnip mash and bake for 20–30 minutes, until crisp and golden.

## Maple-roasted parsnips

SERVES
•
4 AS A
SIDE DISH

Preheat the oven to 180°C (350°F). Peel 1 kg (2 lb 3 oz) parsnips and cut into even-sized pieces. Combine 2 tablespoons olive oil, 1 tablespoon maple syrup and the parsnips in a bowl, mixing well. Season with salt and freshly ground black pepper. Spread the parsnips in a shallow baking dish and roast, turning occasionally, for 45 minutes, or until golden brown and tender.

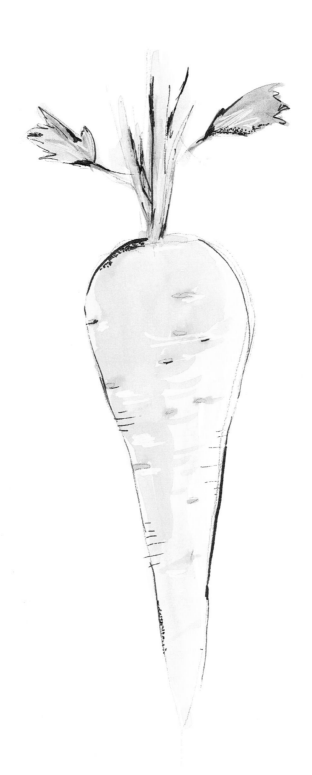

# Spezzatino with root vegetables

Make the most of the cold weather and cook up this warming Italian dish full of the season's best root vegetables. SERVES • 6

OLIVE OIL, FOR COOKING

2 CARROTS, DICED

2 ONIONS, DICED

2 CELERY STALKS, DICED

1.5 KG (3 LB 5 OZ) BRAISING BEEF, SUCH AS BLADE, DICED

2 GARLIC CLOVES, CHOPPED

250 ML (8½ FL OZ/1 CUP) RED WINE

400 G (14 OZ) TINNED CHOPPED TOMATOES

250 ML (8½ FL OZ/1 CUP) TOMATO SUGO

1 BAY LEAF

SALT AND FRESHLY GROUND BLACK PEPPER

250–375 ML (8½–12½ FL OZ/1–1½ CUPS) BEEF STOCK

2 POTATOES, DICED

2 PARSNIPS, CUT INTO 4 EVEN-SIZED PIECES

2 SWEDES (RUTABAGAS), CUT INTO 4 CM (1½ IN) CHUNKS

MASHED POTATO OR CRUSTY BREAD, TO SERVE

Heat a generous splash of olive oil in a large heavy-based saucepan over medium heat. Cook the carrot, onion and celery for 5–6 minutes, until soft but not coloured. Remove from the pan and set aside.

Add more oil if necessary and, working in batches, brown the beef until well sealed. Return the vegetables and all of the beef to the saucepan, along with the garlic, red wine, tomatoes, tomato sugo, bay leaf, salt and freshly ground black pepper, and bring to a gentle simmer.

Add enough stock to ensure the meat is completely covered. Reduce the heat to low and cook, covered, for 1 hour, stirring often. Add the potato, parsnip and swede and continue cooking, covered and stirring frequently, for 1½–2 hours, until the beef and vegetables are tender. Check for seasoning and serve with creamy mashed potato or crusty bread – or both – for mopping up the juices, if desired.

# Fennel

## Fennel and farro salad with pan-fried fish

SERVES
•
4

Put 75 g (2¾ oz/½ cup) farro in a saucepan, cover with water and cook for 10–15 minutes, or until tender. Drain, put in a bowl and allow to cool. Add 3 tablespoons chopped flat-leaf (Italian) parsley, 1 thinly sliced fennel bulb, 200 g (7 oz/1 cup) cooked lentils, 1 tablespoon chopped dill, 2 soaked and finely chopped preserved lemon quarters and 2 tablespoons extra-virgin olive oil. Season with salt and freshly ground black pepper. Heat a splash of oil in a heavy-based frying pan over medium–high heat. Cook 600 g (1 lb 5 oz) firm white fish fillets in batches, for 3–4 minutes on each side, until golden and cooked through. Serve with the farro salad and lemon wedges.

## Salad of fennel, pomegranate and candied walnuts

SERVES
•
4 AS A
SIDE DISH

Make candied walnuts by bringing 500 ml (17 fl oz/2 cups) water and a handful of sugar to the boil. Add 200 g (7 oz/2 cups) walnuts and cook for 3–4 minutes. Drain and allow to dry. Place on a baking tray in a preheated 180°C (350°F) oven for 8 minutes, or until golden. For the salad, take a fennel bulb, remove the tough outer layer and cut in half lengthways. Remove the core and slice the fennel thinly. Put the slices in a large bowl along with several handfuls of salad leaves such as baby English spinach, radicchio and chicory (endive). Add the seeds from ½ pomegranate along with a handful of the candied walnuts and toss to combine. Make a dressing by whisking together 1 tablespoon sherry vinegar, salt and freshly ground black pepper with 3 tablespoons extra-virgin olive oil. Pour over just enough dressing to coat when ready to serve.

# Citrus-cured kingfish with fennel and orange salad

Oily fish such as salmon and kingfish are best for curing. Ask your fishmonger to remove the fine bones that run down the centre of the fish. You can do it yourself if you have tweezers. SERVES • 4–6

1 × 800 G (1 LB 12 OZ) PIECE FIRM WHITE FISH, SKIN ON, SUCH AS KINGFISH, BONES REMOVED

75 G (2¾ OZ) SALT

100 G (3½ OZ) CASTER (SUPERFINE) SUGAR

ZEST OF 2 LEMONS

ZEST OF 2 ORANGES

ZEST OF 2 LIMES

2 FENNEL BULBS

4 ORANGES

80 G (2¾ OZ/½ CUP) PITTED KALAMATA OLIVES, HALVED

1 GENEROUS HANDFUL OF FLAT-LEAF (ITALIAN) PARSLEY

2–3 TABLESPOONS EXTRA-VIRGIN OLIVE OIL

SALT AND FRESHLY GROUND BLACK PEPPER

TOASTED SOURDOUGH BREAD, TO SERVE

**LEMON MAYONNAISE**

125 G (4½ OZ/½ CUP) GOOD-QUALITY MAYONNAISE

ZEST AND JUICE OF 1 LEMON

Place the fish, skin side up, in a deep baking dish. Mix the salt, sugar and zests together and pack the salt–sugar mix onto the fish. Cover with plastic wrap and top with something heavy, such as a bag of rice. Refrigerate for 12 hours. Turn the fish over, re-cover with the plastic wrap and weight, and refrigerate for a further 6 hours.

Remove the fish and discard the salt mixture. Rinse under cold water and pat dry. Starting at the tail and using a sharp knife, slice the fish on an angle into thin slices. You can slice the fish up to 12 hours before it is required; arrange the slices on a tray and place pieces of plastic wrap in between layers. Cover and refrigerate until needed.

To make the lemon mayonnaise, combine the ingredients in a bowl and set aside until needed.

Remove the tough outer layer from the fennel bulbs. Cut them in half lengthways, remove and discard the cores, and slice thinly (use a mandoline if you have one).

Cut the peel and bitter white pith off the oranges with a sharp knife and cut between the membranes to remove each orange segment, catching any juice over a bowl. Combine the orange segments with the sliced fennel, olives and parsley. Whisk the reserved orange juice and the extra-virgin olive oil, and season with salt and freshly ground black pepper. Drizzle over the salad and toss gently.

Serve the fish with the salad and lemon mayonnaise and toasted sourdough on the side.

# Spinach

## Ricotta and spinach gnocchi

SERVES
•
2

Mix 250 g (9 oz/1 cup) ricotta with 1 egg, 50 g (1¾ oz) blanched chopped English spinach, 2 tablespoons grated parmesan and 75 g (2¾ oz/½ cup) plain (all-purpose) flour, and season well with salt and freshly ground black pepper. On a board sprinkled with semolina, roll portions of the mixture into long sausages and then cut into 2 cm (¾ in) lengths. Cook the gnocchi in a large saucepan of boiling salted water for 3–4 minutes, or until the gnocchi float to the surface. Delicious tossed with a tomato, chilli and basil sauce and topped with grated parmesan.

## Spinach and goat's cheese frittata

SERVES
•
8

Blanch 250 g (9 oz) baby English spinach leaves in boiling water. Refresh under cold water, squeeze out excess water and chop roughly. Preheat the oven to 180°C (350°F) and grease a 15 × 20 cm (6 × 8 in) baking dish. Beat together 6 eggs, 125 ml (4 fl oz/½ cup) cream, leaves from 2–3 thyme sprigs, salt and freshly ground black pepper. Mix in the cooked spinach and pour the mixture into the baking dish. Crumble goat's cheese over the top and scatter with 2 tablespoons chopped flat-leaf (Italian) parsley. Bake for 20 minutes, or until puffy and golden. Serve warm.

## Spinach and ricotta fritters

MAKES
•
12–15

Blanch 200 g (7 oz) baby English spinach leaves in boiling water. Refresh under cold water, squeeze out excess water and chop roughly. Beat 2 eggs, add 100 g (3½ oz/⅔ cup) self-raising flour, 60 g (2 oz) polenta, 250 g (9 oz/1 cup) ricotta and the chopped spinach and mix until smooth. Season with salt and freshly ground black pepper. Heat a frying pan over medium–high heat, add a splash of olive oil and 3–4 tablespoonfuls of batter to the pan. Cook for 2–3 minutes on each side, or until golden brown. Turn over and cook for a further 1–2 minutes. Keep fritters warm in a low temperature oven until all the batter mixture is cooked.

# Thai roasted pumpkin, spinach and chickpea curry

This delicious red curry recipe is one you'll go back to again and again. We've been enjoying it for years and it's particularly good in autumn and winter when pumpkins are in season. Economical and warming, this easy meat-free curry is perfect for this time of year. SERVES • 4

750 G (1 LB 11 OZ) PUMPKIN (WINTER SQUASH), PEELED AND CHOPPED INTO 3 CM (1¼ IN) CHUNKS

OLIVE OIL, TO COAT THE PUMPKIN

SALT AND FRESHLY GROUND BLACK PEPPER

125 ML (4 FL OZ/½ CUP) COCONUT CREAM

3 TEASPOONS THAI RED CURRY PASTE

2 TABLESPOONS GRATED PALM SUGAR (JAGGERY)

2 TABLESPOONS FISH SAUCE

500 ML (17 FL OZ/2 CUPS) COCONUT MILK

800 G (1 LB 12 OZ) TINNED CHICKPEAS, DRAINED AND RINSED

100 G (3½ OZ) BABY ENGLISH SPINACH LEAVES

15 G (½ OZ/½ CUP) CORIANDER (CILANTRO) LEAVES, FINELY CHOPPED

Preheat the oven to 180°C (350°F).

Toss the pumpkin in a little olive oil and season with salt and freshly ground black pepper. Place on a baking tray and roast in the oven for 20–30 minutes, or until tender. Set aside.

Heat the coconut cream in a heavy-based saucepan over high heat for a few minutes, until it comes to the boil. Add the curry paste and cook for 20–30 seconds, stirring constantly. Add the palm sugar, fish sauce and coconut milk. Bring the sauce to the boil, then add the roasted pumpkin and chickpeas, and heat through again. Fold in the spinach and cook until the leaves are wilted. Check the seasoning and adjust if necessary.

Garnish with the coriander leaves and serve immediately.

# Caramelised onion and chickpea burgers

These flavour-packed burgers are especially good thanks to the long, slow cooking of the onions. Using dried chickpeas will give you a creamy texture, retain more nutrients and offer superior taste every time, though use tinned if you're short on time. Serve with a little yoghurt tzatziki and a salad with lemon and herb dressing and you have a winner.
SERVES • 3-4

275 G (1 1/4 CUPS) DRIED CHICKPEAS, SOAKED IN COLD WATER OVERNIGHT

80 ML (1/3 CUP) OLIVE OIL

2 ONIONS, SLICED

1 TEASPOON GROUND CUMIN

2 TEASPOONS GROUND CORIANDER

2 TEASPOONS SWEET PAPRIKA

1 TEASPOON MUSTARD SEEDS

1/2 TEASPOON CHILLI POWDER

1 EGG

100–150 G (1–1 1/2 CUPS) DRY BREADCRUMBS

1/2 CUP CHOPPED CORIANDER LEAVES

SALT AND FRESHLY GROUND BLACK PEPPER

VEGETABLE OIL, FOR COOKING

Drain the chickpeas, then place in a large saucepan withplenty of fresh water. Bring to the boil, then cook for 30–40 minutes, or until soft. Drain the chickpeas well, then mash them roughly in a large bowl.

Heat the olive oil in a saucepan, then add the onion, cumin, ground coriander, paprika, mustard seeds and chilli powder. Cook, covered, for at least 20 minutes over low heat, stirring often until the onions soften. Add a little water if it looks dry or begins to catch.

Add the caramelised onion mixture to the chickpeas, along with the egg, breadcrumbs and coriander leaves. Mix well to combine and season to taste. Divide into

12 and form into burgers.

Heat a heavy-based frying pan over a medium heat. Add a splash of vegetable oil and cook the burgers for 5–6 minutes on each side, until golden brown.

# Pumpkin (winter squash)

## Pumpkin and lentil soup

SERVES
•
4

Heat 2 tablespoons oil in a saucepan over medium heat. Cook 1 finely diced onion, 1 thinly sliced leek, 2 finely diced celery stalks and 2 finely diced carrots for 5 minutes, stirring often. Add ¼ finely diced pumpkin (winter squash), 2 crushed garlic cloves, 1 pinch of saffron threads, 1 teaspoon ground coriander, 1 teaspoon ground cumin and 2 teaspoons harissa paste and cook for 2–3 minutes, until fragrant. Add 1 litre (34 fl oz/4 cups) vegetable stock and bring to the boil. Rinse 250 g (9 oz/1 cup) red lentils under cold water and add to the soup. Reduce the heat and cook for 15–20 minutes, or until the lentils are completely tender. Check the seasoning, add 2 tablespoons chopped coriander (cilantro) leaves and serve.

## Chilli-crusted pumpkin and coriander empanadas

MAKES
•
18

Preheat the oven to 180°C (350°F). Season 200 g (7 oz) diced pumpkin (winter squash) with ½ teaspoon chilli flakes, salt and freshly ground black pepper. Put the pumpkin on a baking tray, add enough olive oil to coat and roast until the pumpkin is tender and golden brown. Transfer the pumpkin to a bowl and mash roughly with a fork. Add 100 g (3½ oz) tinned kidney beans (drained and rinsed), 2 tablespoons chopped coriander (cilantro) leaves, the zest and juice of 1 lime, 2 thinly sliced spring onions (scallions), salt and freshly ground black pepper. Cut 2 sheets puff pastry into 9 squares each and put a spoonful of filling in the centre of each. Brush the pastry edges with egg wash, fold to form a triangular parcel and crimp the edges. Transfer to a baking tray and bake for 15–18 minutes, or until the pastry is cooked and golden brown.

# Chipotle-braised beef ribs with spicy baked pumpkin

This is the quintessential winter dish — slow-braised, melting beef — but with a chilli kick to keep things interesting. **SERVES • 4–6**

OIL, FOR COOKING

I ONION, DICED

3–4 GARLIC CLOVES, CHOPPED

2 CINNAMON STICKS

I TEASPOON GROUND CLOVES

I TEASPOON GROUND ALLSPICE

100 G (3½ OZ) TINNED CHIPOTLE CHILLIES IN ADOBO SAUCE

50 G (1¾ OZ/I CUP) CHOPPED CORIANDER (CILANTRO) LEAVES, PLUS EXTRA TO GARNISH

2 TABLESPOONS SOY SAUCE

2 TABLESPOONS BALSAMIC VINEGAR

3 TABLESPOONS SOFT BROWN SUGAR

375 ML (12½ FL OZ/1½ CUPS) TOMATO SUGO

250 ML (8½ FL OZ/I CUP) CHICKEN OR BEEF STOCK

SALT AND FRESHLY GROUND BLACK PEPPER

2 KG (4 LB 6 OZ) BEEF SHORT RIBS

½ TEASPOON CHILLI POWDER, PREFERABLY CHIPOTLE

½ TEASPOON GROUND CORIANDER

½ TEASPOON GROUND CUMIN

I TEASPOON MUSTARD SEEDS, CRUSHED

I LARGE HANDFUL OF CORIANDER (CILANTRO) LEAVES, TO SERVE

**SPICY BAKED PUMPKIN**

1.5 KG (3 LB 5 OZ) PUMPKIN (WINTER SQUASH), PEELED AND CUT INTO WEDGES

OIL, FOR COOKING

SALT AND FRESHLY GROUND BLACK PEPPER

I TABLESPOON CASTER (SUPERFINE) SUGAR

2 TEASPOONS CHILLI FLAKES

Preheat the oven to 180°C (350°F).

Heat a splash of oil in a large heavy-based flameproof casserole dish over medium–high heat. Cook the onion for 3–4 minutes until soft, then add the garlic and cook until fragrant. Add the cinnamon sticks, cloves and allspice and cook for 1–2 minutes, stirring often, before incorporating the chipotle, coriander, soy sauce, balsamic, brown sugar, tomato sugo and stock. Bring to the boil, season well with salt and freshly ground black pepper and allow to simmer for 30 minutes.

Heat a splash of oil in a large heavy-based frying pan over medium–high heat. Working in batches, brown the beef ribs until sealed on all sides and transfer to a large ovenproof dish. Mix together the chilli powder, ground coriander, cumin and mustard seeds. Season well with salt and freshly ground black pepper and sprinkle over the beef, then pour the braising liquid over the seasoned ribs. Cover with foil and bake for 2–3 hours, turning the beef ribs every hour or so.

Meanwhile, to make the spicy baked pumpkin, drizzle the pumpkin with oil, season with salt and freshly ground black pepper and toss with the caster sugar and chilli flakes. Roast for about 2 hours, until tender.

When the ribs are cooked, check for seasoning, scatter with coriander leaves and serve with the baked pumpkin.

# Garlic

## Lemon and garlic-glazed chicken

SERVES
·
4

Mix together the zest and juice of 1 lemon, 1 tablespoon chopped oregano, 2 tablespoons extra-virgin olive oil and 2 crushed garlic cloves. Season with salt and freshly ground black pepper. Rub a whole chicken with the herb mixture. Place the chicken, breast side down, on a wire rack in a roasting tin. Add some water to the tin to stop the fat from burning. Cook in a preheated 180°C (350°F) oven for 45 minutes, or until the skin is crisp. Turn over and cook for a further 30 minutes, until the skin is golden brown and crisp. Check for doneness by inserting a knife into the thickest part of the thigh; the chicken is cooked when the juices run clear, with no trace of pink. Allow to rest for 10 minutes before carving.

## Tunisian sardines with herbs and garlic

SERVES
·
4

Pound 1 handful of coriander (cilantro) leaves and 1 handful of flat-leaf (Italian) parsley using a mortar and pestle. Add 1 teaspoon toasted cumin seeds, 2 garlic cloves and 1 teaspoon salt, then pound until the mixture forms a rough paste. Add 1 teaspoon smoked paprika and 1 tablespoon lemon juice; you may need to add more juice to make a smooth paste. Take 500 g (1 lb 2 oz) butterflied sardines and spread ½ teaspoon of the spice mixture in the middle of each one. Fold the sardines in half so they resemble whole sardines. Heat a splash of oil in a heavy-based frying pan. Lightly coat the sardines in plain (all-purpose) flour, shaking off any excess. Cook the sardines for 2–3 minutes on each side, until golden brown all over. Serve straight away with lemon wedges and a green salad.

# Syrian lamb shanks with ginger and saffron

This is a hearty winter dish with a touch of warmth from the spices and zingy ginger. If you prefer, you can make this recipe with 750 grams (1 lb 11 oz) of diced lamb, but the shanks have more flavour because the meat is cooked on the bone. SERVES • 6

2 TEASPOONS GROUND CUMIN

2 TEASPOONS GROUND CINNAMON

SALT AND FRESHLY GROUND
BLACK PEPPER

6 LAMB SHANKS

2 TABLESPOONS OLIVE OIL

I ONION, THINLY SLICED

10 CM (4 IN) PIECE OF GINGER, PEELED
AND CUT INTO MATCHSTICKS

2 GARLIC CLOVES, CRUSHED

2 SMALL RED CHILLIES, CHOPPED

PINCH OF SAFFRON THREADS

2 TOMATOES, ROUGHLY CHOPPED

2 TABLESPOONS HONEY

100 G (3½ OZ) SLICED DRIED APRICOTS

500 ML (17 FL OZ/2 CUPS) CHICKEN
STOCK

100 G (3½ OZ) COOKED CHICKPEAS

30 G (I OZ/I CUP) CORIANDER
(CILANTRO) LEAVES

STEAMED COUSCOUS, TO SERVE

Preheat the oven to 180°C (350°F).

Combine the cumin and cinnamon in a large bowl with 2 teaspoons of salt and 1 teaspoon of freshly ground black pepper. Lightly coat the lamb shanks with the spice mix.

Heat the olive oil in a large flameproof casserole dish over medium–high heat. Cook the lamb, in batches if necessary, turning often, for about 5 minutes, until golden brown on all sides. Remove from the dish and set aside. Add the onion and ginger and cook for 4–5 minutes, stirring often, until softened. Add the garlic, chilli and saffron, and cook for a further 3 minutes, or until fragrant. Add the tomato and cook for 2–3 minutes. Add the honey and apricots, return the lamb shanks to the dish, and pour in enough stock to cover. Season with salt and bring to the boil. Reduce to a simmer, add the cooked chickpeas and cover with a lid. Transfer to the oven and cook for 2 hours.

Stir in the coriander, check the seasoning and serve with steamed couscous.

# Kale and cavolo nero

## Kale and chorizo with borlotti beans

SERVES
•
4

Prepare 250 g (9 oz) kale by trimming away the tough stems then cut the leaves into thick slices. Heat a large heavy-based saucepan over medium–high heat. Add a splash of olive oil and cook the kale for 3–4 minutes, stirring often until softened. Remove and set aside to cool. Return the pan to the heat, add 2 sliced chorizos and cook for 3–4 minutes on each side, until golden brown. Drain the excess fat away and set aside the chorizo to cool. Meanwhile, make a dressing by puréeing 30 g (1 oz/1 cup) coriander (cilantro) leaves with a pinch of salt and 2 tablespoons olive oil. Combine the kale, chorizo and 150 g (5½ oz) cooked borlotti (cranberry) beans with the dressing and toss to combine. Add salt and freshly ground black pepper to taste and serve.

## Chicken and cavolo nero risotto

SERVES
•
4–6

Heat a large heavy-based saucepan over medium heat. Add 2 tablespoons oil, 1 diced onion, 1 crushed garlic clove, 1 sliced leek and 1 finely diced carrot and cook for 3–4 minutes. Add 500 g (1 lb 2 oz) diced boneless, skinless chicken thighs and cook for 3–4 minutes, or until beginning to brown. Add 300 g (10½ oz) risotto rice and stir briefly. Add 125 ml (4 fl oz/½ cup) white wine and stir until absorbed. Begin adding 750 ml–1 litre (25½–34 fl oz/3–4 cups) hot vegetable or chicken stock – enough to cover the rice at first, then a ladleful at a time until absorbed, stirring well. Cook for 15–20 minutes, until the rice is just done, with each grain slightly firm in the centre. Add 2 handfuls of chopped cavolo nero and cook for 2–3 minutes, until softened. Remove from the heat. Add 35 g (1¼ oz/⅓ cup) finely grated parmesan, 2 tablespoons diced butter and 2 tablespoons chopped flat-leaf (Italian) parsley and stir until creamy. Check for seasoning and serve.

# Red cabbage

## Thai quinoa salad with red cabbage and soy cashews

SERVES
•
4 AS A
SIDE DISH

Bring a saucepan of water to the boil and add 200 g (7 oz/1 cup) quinoa (you can use white, red or black quinoa). Cook for 10–12 minutes, or until the quinoa is cooked. Drain and allow to cool. Meanwhile, to make your own soy cashews bring 500 ml (17 fl oz/2 cups) water, 250 ml (8½ fl oz/1 cup) soy sauce and 115 g (4 oz/½ cup) caster (superfine) sugar to the boil. Add 255 g (9 oz/1⅓ cups) cashews and cook for 2–3 minutes. Drain and spread the cashews out over a baking tray in a single layer. Cook in a preheated 180°C (350°F) oven for 5–6 minutes, or until crisp. Allow to cool before using. Put the quinoa in a large bowl and add 1 grated carrot, ½ diced red capsicum (bell pepper), 75 g (2¾ oz/ 1 cup) shredded red cabbage, 1 handful of pickled ginger, 4 thinly sliced spring onions (scallions), 10 g (¼ oz/⅓ cup) chopped coriander (cilantro) leaves and a handful of the soy cashews. Combine 2 teaspoons coconut sugar, 2 teaspoons fish sauce and 1 tablespoon sweet chilli sauce in a small bowl, then mix through the salad and serve. Delicious on its own or with grilled fish.

## Winter coleslaw

SERVES
•
4 AS A
SIDE DISH

Thinly slice ¼ green cabbage and ¼ red cabbage and put them in a large bowl with 2 grated carrots, 6 finely chopped spring onions (scallions), 2 grated apples, such as granny smith, and 2 tablespoons finely chopped flat-leaf (Italian) parsley. Season well with salt and freshly ground black pepper. When ready to serve, add 2 tablespoons lemon juice and 80 ml (2½ fl oz/⅓ cup) extra-virgin olive oil and toss well to combine. Delicious alongside roast chicken or pork ribs. Feel free to add some fresh sliced chilli to spice things up a bit, or even a handful of chopped pecans for extra crunch.

## Sweet-and-sour braised red cabbage

SERVES
•
4 AS A
SIDE DISH

Melt 2 tablespoons butter in a large heavy-based saucepan over medium heat. Add ½ thinly sliced red cabbage and cook for 3–4 minutes, stirring often. Stir in 80 ml (2½ fl oz/⅓ cup) red wine vinegar and 80 ml (2½ fl oz/⅓ cup) blackcurrant cordial. Cover and cook for 20 minutes, stirring often. Season with salt and freshly ground black pepper.

# Red cabbage and pomegranate slaw

For this salad you need to slice the cabbage, fennel and radish very thinly and evenly; while this is easiest done with a mandoline, it can also be achieved with a sharp knife.
SERVES • 4

1 RED CABBAGE, THINLY SLICED

1 BABY FENNEL BULB, THINLY SLICED

1 BUNCH OF FRENCH BREAKFAST RADISHES, THINLY SLICED

1 POMEGRANATE, SEEDS EXTRACTED

1 HANDFUL OF CHOPPED MINT

1 HANDFUL OF CHOPPED PARSLEY

1 PINK LADY APPLE

JUICE OF 1 LEMON

SALT AND FRESHLY GROUND BLACK PEPPER

2 TABLESPOONS OLIVE OIL

Put the sliced cabbage, fennel and radishes in a bowl. Add the pomegranate seeds, mint and parsley and mix well.

Cut the apple into thin matchsticks and add to a separate small bowl together with the lemon juice. Toss well, then add to the salad. Season well with salt and freshly ground black pepper, add the olive oil and toss well to combine. Serve with any grilled meat or fish.

# Almonds

## Plum and almond cake

SERVES
•
8

Grease and line a 23 cm (9 in) round cake tin and preheat the oven to 180°C (350°F). Cream 125 g (4½ oz) softened butter and 230 g (8 oz/1 cup) caster (superfine) sugar until light and fluffy. Add 2 eggs, one at a time, fully incorporating after each addition. Fold in 125 g (4½ oz/1¼ cups) ground almonds, 225 g (8 oz/1½ cups) self-raising flour, 250 g (9 oz/1 cup) plain yoghurt and 1 teaspoon almond essence. Spoon the mix into the prepared tin. Cut 3 plums into wedges and arrange on top of the cake. Scatter with flaked almonds and bake for 35 minutes, or until a skewer inserted into the cake comes out clean. Allow to cool, then dust with icing (confectioners') sugar to serve.

## Homemade granola

MAKES
•
ROUGHLY 2 KG
(4 LB 6 OZ)

You don't really need a recipe to make granola – just a guideline on quantities of oats to other ingredients. Start with 1.5 kg (3 lb 5 oz) rolled (porridge) oats (never instant oats; they are completely lacking in texture). To this you can add about 3 cups of other ingredients. Perhaps a mix of sultanas (golden raisins), raisins, dried figs, apricots and prunes (these last three ingredients need to be chopped), plus almonds, brazil nuts and sunflower kernels. Simply mix everything together and store in an airtight container. No roasting, no toasting – no work, really. (Of course, you can toast your oats and nuts, but it's easier not to and the result is still completely delicious.) Serve with milk and Greek-style yoghurt.

## Carrot and almond cake with lime frosting

SERVES
•
8–10

Sift 300 g (10½ oz/2 cups) self-raising flour, 1 teaspoon ground cinnamon and 1 teaspoon mixed spice together into a large bowl. Add 4 lightly beaten eggs, 345 g (12 oz/1½ cups) caster (superfine) sugar, 1 teaspoon natural vanilla extract, 310 ml (10½ fl oz/1¼ cups) olive oil and 1 pinch salt. Mix lightly, then incorporate 2 tablespoons chopped almonds, 155 g (5½ oz/1¼ cups) sultanas (golden raisins) and 3 large grated carrots. Pour into a greased and lined 23 cm (9 in) springform cake tin. Bake in a preheated 180°C (350°F) oven for 1 hour, or until a skewer inserted into the cake comes out clean. Meanwhile, to make the lime frosting, put 200 g (7 oz) softened cream cheese, 115 g (4 oz/½ cup) caster (superfine) sugar and the zest and juice of 2 limes in a food processor and blend until smooth. Allow the cake to cool in the tin for 15 minutes, then remove and cool completely on a wire rack. Top with the lime frosting.

# Beetroot (beet)

## Balsamic beetroot

SERVES
•
6 AS A
SIDE DISH

Take 8 beetroot (beets), remove excess leaves and put the beetroot in a saucepan, cover with cold water and bring to the boil. Cook for 30 minutes, or until the beetroot are almost cooked through. Drain and, while still hot, peel the beetroot by holding them under cold water and rubbing the skins off. Cut into wedges and put in a deep roasting tin. Drizzle with 1 tablespoon balsamic vinegar and 3 tablespoons olive oil, add 3–4 thyme sprigs and season well with salt and freshly ground black pepper. Cook in a preheated 180°C (350°F) oven for 30–40 minutes, or until the beetroot are tender. Delicious alongside roast beef.

## Roasted beetroot salad with yoghurt and preserved lemon

SERVES
•
4

Preheat the oven to 180°C (350°F). Choose a deep roasting dish that will fit 4 beetroot (beets) snugly and line it with a double layer of baking paper. Add 4 beetroot, 4–5 thyme sprigs, 2–3 garlic cloves and a good splash of olive oil to the dish. Season well with salt and freshly ground black pepper. Cover with another double layer of baking paper and a layer of foil. Roast for 40–50 minutes, or until the beetroot are cooked. (Depending on the size of the beetroot, it can take a whole hour to roast one. To reduce roasting time by half, parboil the beetroot for 10 minutes before finishing them in the oven.) When cool enough to handle, peel, cut into wedges and put in a bowl with ½ thinly sliced red onion, 1 soaked and finely chopped preserved lemon quarter, 1 tablespoon chopped dill, 2 tablespoons lemon juice, salt and freshly ground black pepper. Combine 125 g (4½ oz/ ½ cup) Greek-style yoghurt with 1 tablespoon tahini, add to the salad and toss lightly to coat.

## Baby beetroot and goat's cheese tart

SERVES
•
4

Remove stems from 4 baby beetroot (beets) and discard. Put the beetroot in a saucepan with 1 cinnamon stick and 1 star anise, cover with water and cook for 10–15 minutes, until tender. Drain and set aside to cool. Once cool, peel and cut into halves. Take a sheet of puff pastry and lay it on a lined baking tray. Brush with olive oil. Cover the pastry with torn rocket (arugula), add the beetroot halves and a handful of crumbled goat's cheese over the top. Season with freshly ground black pepper and drizzle with caramelised balsamic vinegar. Cook in a preheated 200°C (400°F) oven for 15–20 minutes, until the pastry is cooked through and crispy.

# Beetroot soup with basil labne

Rich and restorative, this vibrantly coloured soup is so easy to prepare—simply simmer diced beetroot in an aromatic broth until tender. The addition of basil labne turns it into a luscious winter meal, but you'll need to start the labne a day ahead. **SERVES • 6**

2 TABLESPOONS OLIVE OIL

I ONION, DICED

I CELERY STALK, DICED

I GARLIC CLOVE, CRUSHED

3 MEDIUM BEETROOT (BEETS), PEELED AND CUT INTO I CM (½ IN) DICE

80 ML (2½ FL OZ/⅓ CUP) ORANGE JUICE

I LITRE (34 FL OZ/4 CUPS) CHICKEN STOCK

2 TABLESPOONS BALSAMIC VINEGAR

SALT AND FRESHLY GROUND BLACK PEPPER

**BASIL LABNE**

500 G (I LB 2 OZ/2 CUPS) PLAIN YOGHURT

I TEASPOON SALT

FINELY CHOPPED BASIL LEAVES, FOR COATING

OLIVE OIL, TO COVER (OPTIONAL)

To make the basil labne, place a sieve over a bowl and line with muslin (cheesecloth) or a clean tea towel (dish towel). Mix the yoghurt and salt together. Place the yoghurt in the cloth, then fold the cloth over so the yoghurt is covered. Place the yoghurt (still in the sieve, over the bowl) in the refrigerator and leave to drain overnight.

Divide the labne into small balls using teaspoons. Roll the labne balls in the chopped basil leaves and set aside. (If you want to store them for later use, place the labne balls in a clean jar, cover with olive oil and refrigerate for 3–4 days.)

To make the soup, heat a heavy-based saucepan over medium heat. Add the olive oil, onion and celery and cook for 4–5 minutes, stirring often.

Add the garlic and diced beetroot and cook for a further 5 minutes, stirring often.

Stir in the orange juice, stock and vinegar and bring to the boil. Reduce the heat to low and simmer for 30 minutes, or until the beetroot is tender.

Add salt and lots of freshly ground black pepper, then check the seasoning. Serve each bowl with two or three basil labne balls in the soup.

# Quince

## Quince clafoutis

SERVES
•
4

Put 1 litre (34 fl oz/4 cups) water, 230 g (8 oz/1 cup) caster (superfine) sugar, 1 teaspoon natural vanilla extract and the zest and juice of 1 lemon in a saucepan and bring to a rolling boil. Peel, quarter and core 4 quinces before immediately transferring them to the poaching liquid to prevent discolouration. Reduce the heat and simmer for 1½ hours, or until the quince is tender and ruby-red coloured. Meanwhile, lightly butter an ovenproof dish and preheat the oven to 180°C (350°F). To make clafoutis batter, beat 3 eggs with 80 g (2¾ oz/⅓ cup) caster (superfine) sugar, 250 g (9 oz/1 cup) plain yoghurt, 250 ml (8½ fl oz/1 cup) milk, 2 tablespoons self-raising flour and 1 teaspoon natural vanilla extract. Drain the quinces well and arrange the quarters to cover the base of the buttered dish and pour the batter over the top. Bake for 45 minutes, or until puffed and golden.

## Quince and honey muffins

MAKES
•
6 LARGE OR 12
SMALL MUFFINS

Put 1 litre (34 fl oz/4 cups) water, 230 g (8 oz/1 cup) caster (superfine) sugar, 1 vanilla bean and 2 lemon halves in a saucepan and bring to a rolling boil. Peel, quarter and core 2 quinces before immediately transferring them to the poaching liquid to prevent discolouration. Reduce the heat and simmer for 1½ hours, or until the quince is tender and ruby-red coloured. Drain the quinces well, cut into slices and set them aside. Melt 75 g (2¾ oz) butter and 100 g (3½ oz) honey together. Add 125 ml (4 fl oz/½ cup) milk, 1 egg and 200 g (7 oz/1⅓ cups) self-raising flour. Stir until combined and smooth. Fold through the sliced quince. Spoon the batter into a greased 12- or 6-hole muffin tin. Bake in a preheated 180°C (350°F) oven for 30 minutes, or until risen and golden brown.

## Porridge with poached quince and rhubarb

SERVES
•
4

Put 1 litre (34 fl oz/4 cups) water and 230 g (8 oz/1 cup) caster (superfine) sugar in a saucepan and bring to a rolling boil. Peel, quarter and core 2 quinces before immediately transferring them to the poaching liquid to prevent discolouration. Reduce the heat and simmer for 1½ hours, or until the quince is tender and ruby-red coloured. Drain well. Meanwhile, combine 115 g (4 oz/½ cup) caster sugar with 250 ml (8½ fl oz/1 cup) water in a separate saucepan and bring to the boil over high heat. Reduce the heat, add 250 g (9 oz) rhubarb stalks and cook for 3–4 minutes, stirring occasionally, until the rhubarb is just soft. Remove the rhubarb and allow to cool before using. Put 150 g (5½ oz/1½ cups) rolled (porridge) oats, 500 ml (17 fl oz/2 cups) water and 375 ml (12½ fl oz/1½ cups) milk in a heavy-based saucepan and bring to the boil, stirring occasionally. Reduce the heat and cook for 10–15 minutes, until the porridge reaches the desired consistency. Divide among four bowls and top with the poached quince and rhubarb. Serve with honey on the side.

# Quince and frangipane tart

Frangipane is an almond tart filling that is delicious on its own – and even better poured over seasonal fruit. **SERVES • 8**

230 G (8 OZ/1 CUP) CASTER (SUPERFINE) SUGAR

1 VANILLA BEAN

1 LEMON, HALVED

4 QUINCES

**PASTRY**

200 G (7 OZ/1⅓ CUPS) PLAIN (ALL-PURPOSE) FLOUR, PLUS EXTRA FORDUSTING

100 G (3½ OZ/1 CUP) GROUND ALMONDS

150 G (5½ OZ) SOFTENED BUTTER

PINCH OF SALT

2 EGG YOLKS

3 TABLESPOONS CASTER (SUPERFINE) SUGAR

**FRANGIPANE**

100 G (3½ OZ) SOFTENED BUTTER

115 G (4 OZ/½ CUP) CASTER (SUPERFINE) SUGAR

2 EGGS

75 G (2¾ OZ/¾ CUP) GROUND ALMONDS

1 TABLESPOON PLAIN (ALL-PURPOSE) FLOUR

Put 1 litre (34 fl oz/4 cups) water, the sugar, vanilla bean and lemon halves in a saucepan and bring to a rolling boil over high heat. Peel, quarter and core the quinces before immediately transferring them to the poaching liquid to prevent discolouration. Reduce the heat and simmer for 1½ hours, or until the quinces are tender and ruby-red coloured. Drain the quinces well and set them aside.

For the pastry, rub the flour, ground almonds, butter and salt together until the mixture resembles fine breadcrumbs. Lightly beat the egg yolks and sugar together. Make a well in the centre of the dry ingredients, pour in the egg mixture and knead lightly to form a ball. Wrap in plastic wrap and chill for 30 minutes.

On a lightly floured board, roll out the pastry until it is 3 mm (⅛ in) thick. Line a buttered 25 cm (10 in) flan (tart) tin with the pastry, using your fingers to push it down into the corner. Trim any excess pastry using a small knife. Prick the base of the pastry shell with a fork and return to the refrigerator for another 30 minutes.

Preheat the oven to 180°C (350°F). Line the tart with baking paper and fill it with pastry weights or uncooked rice. Blind bake for 15 minutes before removing the paper and pastry weights or rice and baking for a further 5 minutes to crisp the pastry.

Meanwhile, prepare the frangipane by creaming the butter and sugar until pale and fluffy. Incorporate the eggs, then add the ground almonds and the flour and stir until well combined.

Arrange the poached quince pieces, skin side down, in the cooked pastry shell. Spoon the frangipane over them and return the tart to the oven for 30 minutes, or until the frangipane is set and golden brown.

# Apple

## Baked apples stuffed with walnuts and fig

SERVES
·
6

Put 100 g (3½ oz) thinly sliced dried figs, 125 ml (4 fl oz/½ cup) dessert wine, 1 tablespoon butter and the zest and juice of 1 orange in a saucepan over medium heat. Stir until the liquid comes to the boil then remove from the heat and set aside to cool. When cool, mix with 60 g (2 oz/½ cup) walnut pieces, ½ teaspoon ground nutmeg and ½ teaspoon ground ginger. Remove the cores from 6 apples leaving a wide opening in the tops. Prick the skin with a fork to ensure the apples do not split during cooking. Divide the fig-and-nut mix between the apples, stuffing the mixture into the centre of each apple. Arrange the apples in a buttered baking dish, add 80 ml (2½ fl oz/⅓ cup) water, cover with foil and bake in a preheated 180°C (350°F) oven for 30 minutes. Remove the foil and continue cooking for a further 15 minutes, or until the apples are tender.

## Baby apple cakes

MAKES
·
6

Sift together 100 g (3½ oz/⅔ cup) plain (all-purpose) flour and 1 teaspoon baking powder. Melt 90 g (3 oz) butter with 1 tablespoon mild honey. Put 2 eggs in a food processor with 170 g (6 oz/¾ cup) caster (superfine) sugar, 1 tablespoon soft brown sugar, a pinch of salt and 1 teaspoon natural vanilla extract. Add the melted butter and honey and process until smooth. Add the flour and baking powder and process until combined. Preheat the oven to 180°C (350°F). Butter a 6-hole giant muffin tin and divide the batter among the holes. Core 2 apples and dice into 1 cm (½ in) pieces. Divide the pieces between the cakes. Bake for 15–18 minutes, until firm and golden brown.

## Apple and cinnamon crumble

SERVES
·
6

Peel, core and slice 6 apples, then put the slices in a saucepan along with ½ teaspoon ground cinnamon and 3 tablespoons caster (superfine) sugar. Place over a medium–low heat, cover with a lid and cook for 5 minutes, stirring occasionally. Remove from the heat and set aside. Put 150 g (5½ oz) softened diced butter in a bowl with 155 g (5½ oz/⅔ cup firmly packed) soft brown sugar and 200 g (7 oz/1⅓ cups) plain (all-purpose) flour and rub together until the mixture resembles fine breadcrumbs. Stir through 50 g (1¾ oz/½ cup) rolled (porridge) oats. Put the stewed apple in a baking dish, top with the crumble mixture and bake in a preheated 180°C (350°F) oven for 20 minutes, or until golden brown.

# Apple and quince pie

Custard powder has an interesting effect on pastry. The golden colour it imparts makes for a more aesthetically pleasing dessert, and it adds a flakiness that is lighter than traditional pastry. SERVES • 6–8

345 G (12 OZ/1½ CUPS) CASTER (SUPERFINE) SUGAR, PLUS EXTRA FOR SPRINKLING

I VANILLA BEAN

I LEMON, HALVED

3 QUINCES

3 GRANNY SMITH APPLES

½ TEASPOON GROUND CINNAMON

300 G (10½ OZ/2 CUPS) PLAIN (ALL-PURPOSE) FLOUR

40 G (1½ OZ/⅓ CUP) CUSTARD POWDER

100 G (3½ OZ) ICING (CONFECTIONERS') SUGAR

200 G (7 OZ) UNSALTED BUTTER, DICED

I EGG

Put 1 litre (34 fl oz/4 cups) water, 230 g (8 oz/1 cup) of the caster sugar, the vanilla bean and lemon halves in a saucepan and bring to a rolling boil. Peel, quarter and core the quinces before immediately transferring them to the poaching liquid to prevent discolouration. Reduce the heat and simmer for 1½ hours, or until the quinces are tender and ruby-red coloured. Drain and set aside.

Peel, core and thinly slice the apples. Put in a saucepan with the remaining caster sugar, the cinnamon and 125 ml (4 fl oz/½ cup) water. Bring to the boil over high heat, then reduce the heat and simmer for 5–10 minutes, until the apples are tender but still hold their shape. Slice the quinces into a similar size and mix the two together.

To make the pastry, sift the flour, custard powder and icing sugar together. Rub in the butter to produce a texture resembling breadcrumbs. Add enough water to bring the pastry together and knead briefly. Wrap in plastic wrap and refrigerate for 30 minutes.

Divide the pastry in half and roll one half on a lightly floured work surface to a 3 mm (⅛ in) thickness. Line either a greased 23 cm (9 in) pie dish or shallow flan (tart) tin with the pastry, making sure the pastry is pushed down into the corners. Trim any excess pastry using a small knife and return the pastry to the refrigerator for another 30 minutes. Roll the remaining pastry to the same thickness and refrigerate until needed.

Preheat the oven to 180°C (350°F).

Once chilled, prick the pastry shell with a fork. Line the pastry shell with baking paper and fill it with pastry weights or uncooked rice. Blind bake for 15 minutes before removing the paper and pastry weights or rice and baking for a further 5 minutes to crisp the pastry.

Fill the pastry base with the fruit. Top with the remaining pastry, pressing down the edges and then trimming the excess. Lightly whisk the egg with 2 tablespoons water. Brush the top of the pie with the egg mixture and sprinkle with caster sugar. Bake for 30–40 minutes, or until the pastry is cooked and golden brown.

# Lemon

## Lemon delicious pudding

SERVES
•
4–6

This is a perfect winter dessert that can be made with other citrus fruits: try using limes, oranges or tangelos. Preheat the oven to 180°C (350°F). Butter a 1 litre (34 fl oz/4 cup) pudding bowl and sprinkle with caster (superfine) sugar. Cream 75 g (2¾ oz) softened butter, 345 g (12 oz/1½ cups) caster sugar and the zest of 1 lemon. Add 3 egg yolks, reserving the whites, and mix well. Add 125 ml (4 fl oz/½ cup) lemon juice, 250 ml (8½ fl oz/1 cup) milk and 100 g (3½ oz/⅔ cup) self-raising flour and combine. Beat the egg whites until stiff and fold through the batter. Spoon the mixture into the pudding bowl and put in a deep baking dish. Pour enough hot water into the dish to come halfway up the bowl. Bake for 45 minutes, or until puffed and golden brown.

## Raspberry lemon tart

SERVES
•
6–8

To make sweetcrust pastry, sift 200 g (7 oz/1⅓ cups) plain (all-purpose) flour with a pinch of salt, and rub in 125 g (4½ oz) softened diced butter to produce a breadcrumb texture. Add enough water to bring the dough together (2–3 tablespoons) and knead briefly. Wrap in plastic wrap and chill for 30 minutes before use. Preheat the oven to 180°C (350°F) and grease a 23 cm (9 in) flan (tart) tin. Roll out the pastry to about 5 mm (¼ in) thick and line the tin. Refrigerate for 30 minutes. Prick the pastry with a fork, line it with baking paper and fill with pastry weights or uncooked rice. Blind bake the pastry shell for 15 minutes. Remove the paper and pastry weights or rice and bake for a further 5 minutes to crisp the pastry. When cool, remove the pastry shell from the tin. Combine 250 g (9 oz) good-quality lemon curd with 125 g (4½ oz) mascarpone and pour into the pastry shell. Refrigerate the mixture for at least 4 hours to set. Top with 300 g (10½ oz) fresh raspberries and dust with icing (confectioners') sugar to serve.

## Preserved lemons

MAKES
•
2–3 JARS

Cut 8 lemons into quarters. Put 4 tablespoons salt, 2–3 cloves and 1 cinnamon stick in a large saucepan of water and bring to the boil. When boiling, add half of the lemon quarters and allow the water to return to the boil, cooking for 7–8 minutes. Remove the lemon quarters, drain, and repeat with the next batch. Reserve the cooking liquid. Squash the lemons into sterilised glass jars and push down firmly. When each jar is full, cover the lemons with the reserved cooking liquid. Store in a cool, dark place for 3–4 weeks before using. To use the preserved lemons soak a wedge in cold water for 10 minutes, cut out and discard the pulpy centre and use the lemon rind in your recipe.

# Lemon olive oil cake with raspberry curd

This is a delightful afternoon-tea cake. The curd recipe makes enough for two cakes, so you can either make this cake again or enjoy the curd by smearing on fresh crusty bread.
SERVES • 8

190 ML (6½ FL OZ/¾ CUP) LIGHT OLIVE OIL

2 EGGS

FINELY GRATED ZEST OF 2 LEMONS

150 ML (5 FL OZ) LEMON JUICE

250 G (9 OZ/1 CUP) PLAIN YOGHURT

345 G (12 OZ/1½ CUPS) CASTER (SUPERFINE) SUGAR

300 G (10½ OZ/2 CUPS) SELF-RAISING FLOUR

250 ML (8½ FL OZ/1 CUP) WHIPPING CREAM

300 G (10½ OZ) FRESH RASPBERRIES

**RASPBERRY CURD**

4 EGG YOLKS

230 G (8 OZ/1 CUP) CASTER (SUPERFINE) SUGAR

200 G (7 OZ) BUTTER, SOFTENED

FINELY GRATED ZEST OF 2 LEMONS

80 ML (2½ FL OZ/⅓ CUP) LEMON JUICE

210 G (7⅓ OZ/1⅓ CUPS) FRESH RASPBERRIES

**RASPBERRY ICING (FROSTING)**

115 G (4 OZ/½ CUP) CASTER (SUPERFINE) SUGAR

210 G (7⅓ OZ/1⅓ CUPS) FRESH RASPBERRIES

125–185 G (4½–6½ OZ/1–1½ CUPS) ICING (CONFECTIONERS') SUGAR

To make the raspberry curd, beat the egg yolks and sugar in a large heatproof bowl until pale and creamy. Add the butter, lemon zest and juice. Place over a simmering saucepan of water and whisk continuously for 20–30 minutes, until thickened. Remove from the heat and stir the raspberries through, allowing the fruit to break up. Allow to cool, then store in the refrigerator for up to 2 weeks, until required.

Preheat the oven to 180°C (350°F). Grease a 23 cm (9 in) round cake tin or a loaf (bar) tin.

Put the olive oil, eggs, lemon zest and juice, yoghurt and sugar in a bowl and whisk to combine. Sift in the flour and stir until smooth. Pour the mixture into the prepared cake tin and bake for 35 minutes, or until a skewer inserted into the cake centre of the cake comes out clean. Remove from the oven and allow to cool.

Meanwhile, to make the raspberry icing, combine the caster sugar with 125 ml (4 fl oz/½ cup) water in a saucepan over low heat, stirring until the sugar dissolves. Bring to the boil. Remove from the heat and allow to cool. Put the raspberries in a food processor and slowly add the cooled sugar syrup until you have a thick sauce (you may not need all the sugar syrup). Transfer to a bowl and stir in the icing sugar until thick and well combined.

Whip the cream until soft peaks form. Put half the curd in a large bowl and stir until it is malleable. Mix in a spoonful of the whipped cream. Add the remaining cream and gently fold through to make a light, airy mousse. Spread the mousse over the cooled cake. Top with the raspberry icing and fresh raspberries, and serve.

# Lamb

## Sweet and sticky lamb ribs

SERVES
6

Mix together 80 ml (2½ fl oz/⅓ cup) olive oil, 1 tablespoon ground cumin, 1 tablespoon ground coriander, 1 tablespoon smoked paprika, 2 crushed garlic cloves, salt and freshly ground black pepper. Pour the mixture over 2 kg (4 lb 6 oz) lamb ribs, using your fingers to coat them well. Marinate in the fridge for up to 4 hours. Preheat the oven to 160°C (320°F). Place the ribs on a roasting rack over a baking dish and bake for 2 hours, turning occasionally. Mix together 2 tablespoons brown sugar, 2 tablespoons fish sauce and 1 tablespoon tamarind purée. Remove the lamb from the oven, cut each section into individual ribs, return to the wire rack and baste with the glaze. Turn oven up to 180°C (350°F) and cook the ribs another 20–30 minutes, basting and turning occasionally, until golden brown and crisp. Serve with lemon wedges and mashed potato.

## Chilli–mint lamb cutlets

SERVES
6–8

Make a marinade by mixing together 2 seeded and finely chopped small red chillies, 2 tablespoons finely chopped mint, 1 crushed garlic clove, the zest of 1 lemon, 2 tablespoons olive oil, salt and freshly ground black pepper. Allow 3–4 lamb cutlets per person and marinate for up to 4 hours. Cook the lamb cutlets on a hot barbecue for 4 minutes. Turn over and cook for a further 3–4 minutes. Serve immediately.

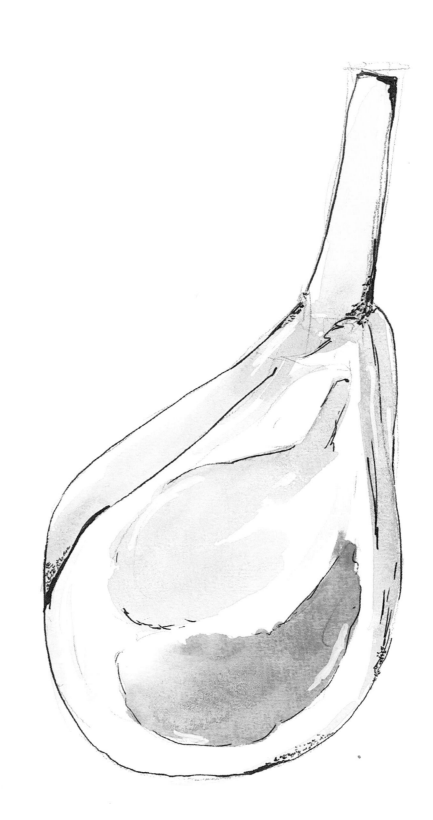

# Herb-roasted leg of lamb with hot broad bean and feta dressing

Lamb, feta and herbs are a perfect combination. Try to cook the lamb so it's still pink in the middle and allow to rest for a good 15 minutes before carving. SERVES • 6

2 GARLIC CLOVES

2 TABLESPOONS CHOPPED OREGANO

2 TABLESPOONS CHOPPED ROSEMARY

2 TABLESPOONS CHOPPED BASIL

ZEST OF 2 LEMONS

125 ML (4 FL OZ/½ CUP) OLIVE OIL

SALT AND FRESHLY GROUND
BLACK PEPPER

1.5 KG (3 LB 5 OZ) LAMB LEG

1.5 KG (3 LB 5 OZ) BROAD (FAVA) BEANS

80 G (2¾ OZ/½ CUP) PITTED
KALAMATA OLIVES

1 HANDFUL OF FLAT-LEAF (ITALIAN)
PARSLEY

1 SMALL HANDFUL OF MINT,
ROUGHLY TORN

2 TABLESPOONS LEMON JUICE

1 TEASPOON DIJON MUSTARD

3 TABLESPOONS EXTRA-VIRGIN OLIVE OIL

100 G (3½ OZ) CRUMBLED FETA

Preheat the oven to 180°C (350°F).

Grind the garlic using a mortar and pestle. Add the herbs and lemon zest and grind to a rough paste. Add the olive oil, season with salt and freshly ground black pepper and mix until combined.

Rub the herb-and-garlic paste all over the lamb. Place in a deep roasting tin and roast for 1–1½ hours. To check if the lamb is done, insert a small knife into the centre of the roast. Count to five. If the knife feels warm (tepid), the meat is rare. If it feels bearably hot, the meat is medium. You're aiming for medium to medium-rare. If necessary, cook for a further 5 minutes and test again. Cover and rest for 20 minutes in a warm place before carving.

Meanwhile, remove the broad beans from their pods and bring a large saucepan of water to the boil. Cook the beans for 1 minute, then drain and refresh under cold water. Remove the pale green skins by creating a slit in the skin and pushing the beans through it. Discard the skins.

Toss the broad beans, olives, parsley and mint together in a bowl. In a separate bowl, whisk together the lemon juice, mustard and extra-virgin olive oil, and season with salt and freshly ground black pepper. Pour into a large frying pan over medium–low heat, add the feta and the broad-bean mixture, and cook gently until just warmed through. Pour the lamb roasting-pan juices into the dressing and stir to combine. Remove from the heat.

To serve, carve the lamb and top with the hot broad bean and feta dressing.

# Peas

## Pea and asparagus salad with feta and prosciutto

SERVES
·
4

Cook 6 prosciutto slices in a large frying pan over medium–high heat for 2–3 minutes on each side until crisp. Drain on paper towel. Bring a saucepan of water to the boil and cook 180 g (6½ oz) asparagus for 1–2 minutes. Remove and refresh under cold water before discarding the woody ends and cutting the spears into 3 cm (1¼ in) pieces. Cook 150 g (5½ oz) fresh peas and 150 g (5½ oz) snow peas (mangetout) in the boiling water for 1–2 minutes; drain and refresh. Combine the asparagus, peas and snow peas in a large bowl with 3 tablespoons toasted pine nuts, 3 tablespoons mint leaves, 10 g (¼ oz/½ cup) flat-leaf (Italian) parsley, 50 g (1¾ oz) snow pea (mangetout) sprouts and 50 g (1¾ oz) rocket (arugula). Make a honey dressing by mixing 1 tablespoon red wine vinegar and ½ teaspoon dijon mustard together. Season with salt and freshly ground black pepper. Add 1 teaspoon honey and 3 tablespoons extra-virgin olive oil and whisk to combine. Dress the salad with the honey dressing and toss to combine just before serving. Arrange on a platter, scatter 100 g (3½ oz) crumbled feta over the top and add the crumbled crisp prosciutto slices.

## Pea and mint croquettes

MAKES
·
12

Bring a large saucepan of water to the boil and cook 700 g (1 lb 9 oz/4½ cups) fresh peas until tender. Drain and refresh under cold water. Heat a small pan over medium heat, add a splash of oil and cook 1 diced onion until soft. Add 2 crushed garlic cloves and cook for a further 1–2 minutes. Put the cold peas in a food processor and blitz until well chopped but not mushy. Put in a bowl along with 230 g (8 oz/1 cup) mashed potato, 1 handful of finely chopped mint and the cooked onion and garlic. Season well with salt and freshly ground black pepper. Mix well. Shape into 12 croquettes and put in the refrigerator to chill. Coat each croquette with seasoned flour, beaten egg and panko breadcrumbs. Deep-fry until golden brown.

## Mixed pea salad

SERVES
·
4 AS A
SIDE DISH

Bring a saucepan of water to the boil. Blanch a big handful of snow peas (mangetout) for 1 minute, drain and refresh. Take 500 g (1 lb 2 oz) fresh peas and blanch for 2–3 minutes, until tender. Drain and refresh. Take the snow peas and cut thinly lengthways, then put them in a large bowl along with the cooked peas, 100 g (3½ oz) snow pea (mangetout) sprouts and a handful of watercress, rocket (arugula) or other dark green leaf. Try also adding other spring vegetables such as asparagus, broad (fava) beans, sugar snap peas or green beans for more texture. Make a simple dressing with 1 tablespoon lemon juice, 2 teaspoons honey, 3 tablespoons olive oil, salt and freshly ground black pepper. Toss the salad with just enough dressing to coat and serve with crumbled feta on top.

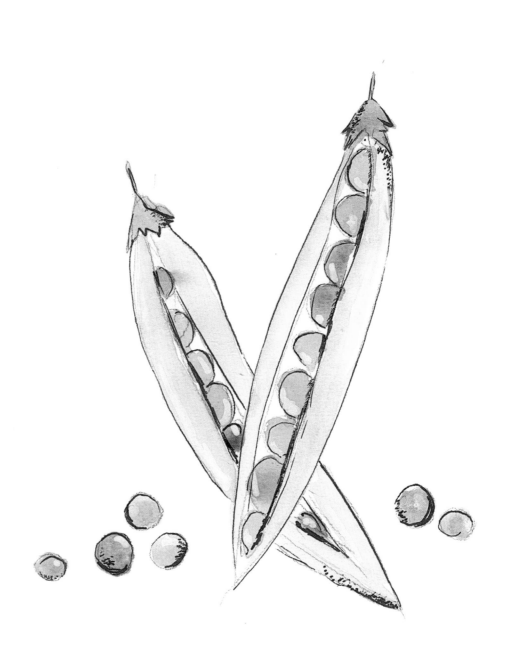

# Moroccan broad bean salad with yoghurt and crispy breadcrumbs

This is a simple dish, but one that requires quality ingredients. All the stages can be prepared in advance and then assembled just before serving. Make sure you serve the broad beans and breadcrumbs either slightly warm or at room temperature. SERVES • 4

2 TEASPOONS CUMIN SEEDS

1 TEASPOON CORIANDER SEEDS

250 G (9 OZ) SOURDOUGH BREAD, CRUSTS REMOVED

OIL, FOR COOKING

1 KG (2 LB 3 OZ) BROAD (FAVA) BEANS

1 LEMON

250 G (9 OZ/1 CUP) PLAIN YOGHURT

2 TEASPOONS TAHINI

2 TABLESPOONS CHOPPED CORIANDER (CILANTRO) LEAVES OR MINT, OR BOTH

SALT AND FRESHLY GROUND BLACK PEPPER

1 RED ONION, FINELY SLICED

3 TABLESPOONS EXTRA-VIRGIN OLIVE OIL

2 TABLESPOONS SHREDDED MINT

Heat a small frying pan over medium heat and toast the cumin seeds until golden brown and fragrant. Remove and set aside to cool. Repeat with the coriander seeds. Once cool, grind them roughly using a mortar and pestle. Set aside.

Roughly chop the sourdough bread into breadcrumbs. Heat a large heavy-based frying pan over medium–high heat. Add a generous splash of oil and the breadcrumbs and cook for 4–5 minutes, stirring often, until the breadcrumbs are golden and crunchy. When just about cooked, sprinkle the ground spices over the top and toss well to coat the breadcrumbs.

Remove the broad beans from their pods and bring a large saucepan of water to the boil. Cook the beans for 1 minute, then drain and refresh under cold water. Remove the pale green skins by creating a slit in the skin and pushing the beans through it. Discard the skins. Put the bright green inner beans in a bowl.

In a separate bowl, finely grate the zest of the lemon and combine with the yoghurt, tahini, coriander and/or mint. Season well with salt and freshly ground black pepper and set aside.

Juice the lemon and add to the broad beans, along with the red onion, olive oil and mint. Leave at room temperature until ready to serve.

To serve, divide the yoghurt mixture among four bowls, top with the broad beans and scatter with the crispy breadcrumbs.

# Asparagus

## Leek and asparagus tart

SERVES
•
6

Preheat the oven to 180°C (350°F) and grease a 23 cm (9 in) flan (tart) tin. Trim 2 leeks. Cut in half lengthways, rinse well then thinly slice. Heat 2 tablespoons butter in a large heavy-based frying pan over medium heat. Add the leeks and cook slowly, stirring often, until soft. Season well. Cut 10–12 sheets filo pastry into squares slightly larger than the tin. Brush each sheet with melted butter and layer them in the tin. Put the leeks in the base of the pastry-lined tin. Mix 250 g (9 oz) goat's curd or ricotta with 3 tablespoons cream, 3 eggs, the zest of 1 lemon, 2 tablespoons chopped mint and 2 tablespoons chopped flat-leaf (Italian) parsley, and season with salt and freshly ground black pepper. Pour the mix into tin and top with 200 g (7 oz) chopped asparagus spears. Bake for 25–30 minutes, until set and golden.

## Thai prawn and asparagus curry

SERVES
•
4

Cook 140 ml (4½ fl oz) coconut cream in a heavy-based saucepan over medium–high heat for 5 minutes. When the coconut cream separates and the oil floats on the surface, add 3 tablespoons Thai red curry paste and cook for 5 minutes, stirring constantly, until fragrant. Add 1 tablespoon grated palm sugar (jaggery) and cook briefly before adding 2 tablespoons fish sauce and 400 ml (13½ fl oz) coconut milk. Bring the liquid to the boil, then reduce the heat and simmer for 8–10 minutes. Add 500 g (1 lb 2 oz) peeled and deveined raw prawns (shrimp), 150 g (5½ oz) chopped asparagus and ½ thinly sliced red capsicum (bell pepper). Return to the boil, then reduce the heat and simmer for 2–3 minutes, or until the prawns are cooked. Add coriander (cilantro) leaves to taste, check for seasoning and serve with jasmine rice.

## Asparagus tortilla

SERVES
•
2

Snap off the bases from 180 g (6½ oz) asparagus spears and cut each spear into 3–4 pieces. Heat a small frying pan over medium heat and add a splash of olive oil and the asparagus. Pan-fry, stirring gently, for 4–5 minutes. Beat 5 eggs with a generous sprinkle of salt flakes. Pour the egg over the asparagus and reduce the heat to low. Allow the tortilla to set on the base of the pan, but gently loosen the edges by running a small knife around them. When the tortilla is set, slide it onto a plate and allow to cool. Cut into wedges.

# Spaghetti with smoked trout and asparagus

This silky sauce celebrates the season with tender, vibrant asparagus and sweet, smoked trout. Be sure to add a generous pinch of salt to the spaghetti water – this helps season the pasta while cooking and gives it extra flavour. SERVES • 6

400 G (14 OZ) SPAGHETTI

3 TABLESPOONS OLIVE OIL

1 ONION, CHOPPED

1 GARLIC CLOVE, CRUSHED

1 WHOLE SMOKED TROUT, SKIN AND BONES REMOVED, FLAKED

250 ML (8½ FL OZ/1 CUP) CHICKEN STOCK

200 G (7 OZ) ASPARAGUS, CUT INTO 2 CM (¾ IN) LENGTHS

40 G (1½ OZ) BUTTER

SALT AND FRESHLY GROUND BLACK PEPPER

2 TABLESPOONS CHOPPED FLAT-LEAF (ITALIAN) PARSLEY

Bring a large saucepan of water to the boil over high heat. Add a good pinch of salt. Add the pasta to the boiling water and stir until the water has returned to the boil. Reduce the heat, cover and cook the pasta at a fast simmer for 8 minutes.

Meanwhile, heat a frying pan over medium–high heat. Add the olive oil and onion and cook for 3–4 minutes, stirring often, until the onion softens slightly. Add the garlic and cook for a further 1–2 minutes, or until fragrant.

Add the smoked trout and stock and bring to the boil, then add the asparagus and cook for 2–3 minutes, or until the asparagus is tender. Remove the pan from the heat and add the butter, salt and lots of freshly ground black pepper. Gently stir together, then add the parsley. Drain the pasta and toss with the sauce to serve.

# Crab, green mango and asparagus salad

Green mango is delicious in this recipe, as the unripe fruit provides astringency and a crisp texture to the salad. To peel a mango, stand it upright and, using a sharp knife, remove the skin, following the natural shape of the mango. SERVES • 6

500 G (1 LB 2 OZ) ASPARAGUS SPEARS, TRIMMED AND CUT INTO 3 CM (1¼ IN) PIECES

1 TELEGRAPH (LONG) CUCUMBER, PEELED, CUT IN HALF LENGTHWAYS, SEEDED AND THINLY SLICED ON AN ANGLE

1 GREEN MANGO, PEELED AND THINLY SLICED

20 G (¾ OZ/1 CUP) MINT, OR A COMBINATION OF MINT AND VIETNAMESE MINT

30 G (1 OZ/1 CUP) CORIANDER (CILANTRO) LEAVES

2 KAFFIR LIME LEAVES, FINELY SHREDDED

75 G (2¾ OZ/2½ CUPS) PICKED WATERCRESS

2 TABLESPOONS PICKLED GINGER

1 TABLESPOON FISH SAUCE

2 TABLESPOONS LIME JUICE

1 SMALL RED CHILLI, SEEDED AND FINELY CHOPPED

1 TABLESPOON GRATED PALM SUGAR (JAGGERY)

FRESHLY GROUND BLACK PEPPER

250 G (9 OZ) FRESH CRABMEAT

Blanch the asparagus in boiling water for 2–3 minutes, then refresh under cold water.

Combine the asparagus, cucumber, mango, mint, coriander, kaffir lime leaves, watercress and pickled ginger in a large bowl.

Combine the fish sauce and lime juice in a small bowl. Add the chilli and palm sugar and stir until the sugar is dissolved. Season with freshly ground black pepper.

When ready to serve, toss the salad ingredients with the dressing and divide among six plates. Top with the crabmeat and serve.

# Ginger

## Ginger chicken stir-fry with broccolini

SERVES
·
4

Slice 2 boneless, skinless chicken breasts into thin strips. Prepare marinade by mixing together 3 tablespoons soy sauce, 3 tablespoons Chinese rice wine, 2 teaspoons sesame oil, 2 teaspoons caster (superfine) sugar and 2 tablespoons grated ginger. Pour over the chicken and allow to marinate for 20 minutes. Remove the chicken from the marinade, reserving the liquid. Heat a wok until hot, add a splash of oil and stir-fry the chicken strips for 2–3 minutes, until browned. Add 125 ml (4 fl oz/½ cup) chicken stock and 1–2 tablespoons of the reserved marinade. Add 200 g (7 oz) chopped broccolini and cook for a further 3–4 minutes, stirring often. Serve with steamed rice.

## Ginger-lime glazed chicken

SERVES
·
4

Preheat the oven to 180°C (350°F). Put 1 kg (2 lb 3 oz) chicken (whole or pieces) in a roasting dish. Rub with a splash of olive oil and sprinkle with chilli flakes, salt and freshly ground black pepper. Roast for 30–40 minutes, turning often. Meanwhile, prepare the glaze by whisking together 2 tablespoons honey, 1 tablespoon grated ginger and the zest and juice of 1 lime. Pour over the chicken and continue roasting until golden brown and cooked through. Scatter with coriander (cilantro) leaves and serve with lime wedges and steamed rice.

## Rhubarb and ginger relish

MAKES
·
500 ML (17 FL OZ/
2 CUPS)

Cut 400 g (14 oz) rhubarb into 2 cm (¾ in) pieces and put in a saucepan along with 1 seeded and finely chopped small red chilli, 2 teaspoons grated ginger, 2 cinnamon sticks, 1 star anise, 2–3 bruised cardamom pods, 115 g (4 oz/½ cup) caster (superfine) sugar and 80 ml (2½ fl oz/⅓ cup) white vinegar. Bring to the boil, stirring often, then reduce the heat to low and cook for 20–30 minutes, until the relish reaches setting point. (Drop a teaspoon of relish onto a chilled plate. Tip the plate. If relish doesn't run it has reached setting point.) Pour into sterilised glass jars while still hot.

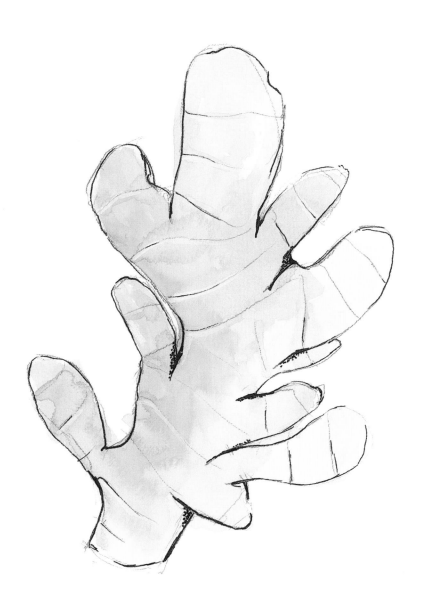

# Slow-roasted tikka lamb with cucumber salsa

Roasting this lamb for 5 hours will ensure that the meat is beautifully tender and falls off the bone, and that the tikka paste gets absorbed into the meat. SERVES • 6

2 KG (4 LB 6 OZ) LAMB SHOULDER, BONE-IN

4 HEAPED TABLESPOONS TIKKA PASTE (SEE BELOW)

2 LONG RED CHILLIES, SLICED

4 GARLIC CLOVES, SLICED

2–3 MINT SPRIGS, LEAVES PICKED

OLIVE OIL, FOR COOKING

500 ML (17 FL OZ/2 CUPS) CHICKEN STOCK

## TIKKA PASTE

I TEASPOON GROUND CUMIN

I TEASPOON GROUND CORIANDER

2 GARLIC CLOVES

THUMB-SIZED PIECE OF GINGER, PEELED

I TEASPOON CAYENNE PEPPER

I TABLESPOON SMOKED PAPRIKA

2 TEASPOONS GARAM MASALA

3 TABLESPOONS OIL

2 TABLESPOONS TOMATO PASTE (CONCENTRATED PURÉE)

2 RED CHILLIES

80 G (2¾ OZ) CORIANDER (CILANTRO) LEAVES AND STEMS

2 TABLESPOONS DESICCATED (SHREDDED) COCONUT

## CUCUMBER SALSA

I CUCUMBER, PEELED

4 FRENCH SHALLOTS, THINLY SLICED

30 G (I OZ/I CUP) CORIANDER (CILANTRO) LEAVES

I SMALL RED CHILLI, SEEDED AND SLICED

I TABLESPOON LIME JUICE

2 TABLESPOONS OLIVE OIL

SALT AND FRESHLY GROUND BLACK PEPPER

To make the tikka paste, put all the ingredients in a food processor and blend until smooth.

Lightly score the fat side of the lamb all over with a sharp knife, then stab it a few times and use your fingers to make little holes. Spread the tikka paste over the lamb and into the holes, and then stuff the holes with slices of chilli and garlic and the mint leaves. Cover and marinate in the refrigerator overnight.

When ready to cook, preheat the oven to 170°C (340°F). Take the marinated lamb out of the refrigerator and let it come to room temperature. Put the lamb in a deep roasting tin, drizzle with olive oil and add the stock. Cover with a sheet of baking paper and a sheet of foil.

Roast the lamb, basting it occasionally, for 4–5 hours, or until the coating is dark and the meat is beautifully tender. Remove the lamb from the tin and leave to rest. When ready to serve, tear the lamb into pieces with two forks.

Meanwhile, to make the cucumber salsa, use a vegetable peeler to cut long ribbons from the cucumber. Discard the seeds and squeeze any excess moisture out of the cucumber strips. Put them in a bowl, along with the shallots, coriander and chilli. Add the lime juice and olive oil and season to taste. Serve the lamb on a large platter with the cucumber salsa alongside it.

# Coriander (cilantro)

## Stir-fried corn with chorizo and coriander

SERVES
·
4 AS A
SIDE DISH

Remove the husks and silky tassels from 3 corn cobs. Rinse. Using a sharp knife, cut down the length of the cobs, removing all the kernels but taking care not to remove too much of the starchy core. Set aside. Heat a heavy-based frying pan over medium–high heat and add 1 tablespoon olive oil and 2 sliced chorizo, cooking for 5–6 minutes, or until golden brown. Drain the excess fat away and set the chorizo aside. Return the pan to the heat and add 1 tablespoon oil along with the reserved corn kernels, 6 thinly sliced spring onions (scallions) and 1 diced red capsicum (bell pepper). Cook for 2–3 minutes, until softened, then return the chorizo to the pan. Cook for 2–3 minutes, stirring often. Add 1 handful of chopped coriander (cilantro) leaves, the juice of 1 lime and season well with salt and freshly ground black pepper.

## Coriander salmon tacos

SERVES
·
2–4

Remove and discard the skin and any brown flesh from a 200 g (7 oz) sashimi-grade salmon fillet and dice finely. Mix with the zest of 1 lime, 2 thinly sliced spring onions (scallions) and 2 tablespoons chopped coriander (cilantro) leaves, then season with salt and freshly ground black pepper. Mash 1 avocado with 2 tablespoons lemon juice, stir in 2 tablespoons chopped coriander (cilantro) leaves and a dash of Tabasco sauce if desired. Warm 4 soft tortillas in the microwave, or wrap in foil and cook in a preheated 180°C (350°F) oven for 3–4 minutes. Divide the salmon and avocado among the tortillas and serve.

# Chilli

## Twice-cooked chilli and tamarind pork ribs

SERVES
•
4

To make tamarind water, soak 1 tablespoon tamarind pulp in 125 ml (4 fl oz/½ cup) boiling water for 10–15 minutes. Work the tamarind flesh off the seeds with your fingers and strain, keeping the juices. Cut 1 kg (2 lb 3 oz) pork ribs into sections and put in a large wide-based saucepan. Bring to the boil over medium heat with 125 ml (4 fl oz/½ cup) of the tamarind water, 2–3 garlic cloves, 2 cinnamon sticks, ½ teaspoon ground cloves, ½ teaspoon ground allspice, 2 chipotle chillies in adobo sauce, 1 diced onion, 50 g (1¾ oz/1 cup) chopped coriander (cilantro) roots and all, 1 tablespoon balsamic vinegar, 3 tablespoons soft brown sugar, 400 g (14 oz) tinned chopped tomatoes and enough water to cover. Reduce the heat, cover and cook for 40 minutes, or until the ribs are tender. Preheat the oven to 180°C (350°F). Transfer the ribs to a baking tray, brush with oil and bake for 20–30 minutes, turning every 5 minutes, until golden brown all over. Purée the cooking liquid and bring back to a gentle simmer. Check for seasoning, pour over the cooked ribs and garnish with coriander leaves (cilantro). Serve with steamed rice.

## Linguine vongole

SERVES
•
4

Bring a large saucepan of salted water to the boil over high heat. Add 400 g (14 oz) linguine and stir until the water returns to the boil. Reduce the heat, cover and cook the pasta for 8 minutes. Heat a large heavy-based frying pan over medium heat. Add 2 tablespoons olive oil, 2 crushed garlic cloves, 2 seeded and finely chopped small red chillies and cook for 1–2 minutes, until fragrant. Add 80 ml (2½ fl oz/⅓ cup) white wine, bring to the boil and cook until reduced by half. Add 125 ml (4 fl oz/½ cup) chicken stock and bring to a simmer. Add 500 g (1 lb 2 oz) rinsed pipis or clams. Discard any pipis or clams that do not open. Cook for 2–3 minutes, stirring often, until all the pipis or clams open. Drain and add the pasta along with 2 tablespoons butter and 2 tablespoons chopped flat-leaf (Italian) parsley. Season well with freshly ground black pepper, toss to combine and serve.

# Mexican corn fritters with guacamole

These spiced fritters make the perfect partner to a smooth, creamy guacamole laced with spring onion and herbs and are good served at any time of day. SERVES • 4

1 TEASPOON GROUND CUMIN

1 TEASPOON GROUND CORIANDER

¼ TEASPOON SMOKED PAPRIKA

2 TEASPOONS CHOPPED CHIPOTLE IN ADOBO SAUCE

75 G (2¾ OZ/½ CUP) SELF-RAISING FLOUR

150 G (5½ OZ/1 CUP) POLENTA

½ TEASPOON SALT

1 TEASPOON BAKING POWDER

1 EGG

250 ML (8½ FL OZ/1 CUP) MILK

2 CORN COBS

1–2 TABLESPOONS OIL

ROCKET (ARUGULA), TO SERVE

**GUACAMOLE**

1 RIPE AVOCADO

2 TABLESPOONS LIME JUICE

2 TABLESPOONS CHOPPED CORIANDER (CILANTRO) LEAVES

A DASH OR TWO OF TABASCO SAUCE

1 TOMATO, FINELY DICED

2 SPRING ONIONS (SCALLIONS), THINLY SLICED

SALT AND FRESHLY GROUND BLACK PEPPER

In a large bowl, combine the cumin, ground coriander, smoked paprika, chipotle, flour, polenta, salt, baking powder, egg and milk. Mix until smooth. Allow to stand for 10 minutes; if necessary, add more liquid.

Meanwhile, make the guacamole. Cut the avocado in half by using a sharp knife to cut around the stone, then twist to separate. Remove the stone carefully using the heel of the knife and discard. Holding each avocado half in the palm of your hand, use a small knife to roughly crisscross the flesh and scoop into a bowl. Add the lime juice, coriander, Tabasco, tomato and spring onion. Season with salt and freshly ground black pepper. Mix to combine, making it as chunky or as smooth as you prefer.

Remove the kernels from the corn cobs and add to the batter.

Heat the oil in a heavy-based frying pan over medium heat. Drop spoonfuls of the batter into the pan and cook on one side until golden brown with bubbles forming on top. Turn the fritters over and cook the other side until golden brown. Repeat until the mixture is used up, adding more oil as needed and keeping cooked fritters warm in the oven.

To serve, top the fritters with rocket and guacamole and serve while still warm.

# Barbecued chicken with fresh mango salsa

This is a brilliant marinade for chicken and we hope it inspires you to get the barbecue fired up. You will need a hood on your barbecue or be able to improvise a lid to cook these chicken pieces. The marinade is a simple combination of lime juice, fresh chilli and Spanish paprika, which adds a wonderful flavour and colour to the meat. The mango salsa adds a sweet and lively reminder that spring is here! SERVES • 4

1.6 KG (3½ LB) WHOLE CHICKEN, CUT INTO 8 PIECES

2 GARLIC CLOVES, CRUSHED

1 TABLESPOON SMOKED PAPRIKA

1 SMALL RED CHILLI, FINELY CHOPPED

125 ML (4 FL OZ/½ CUP) LIME JUICE (ABOUT 3 LIMES)

2 TABLESPOONS OLIVE OIL

2 TEASPOONS SHERRY VINEGAR

1 TEASPOON CASTER (SUPERFINE) SUGAR

**MANGO SALSA**

1 RIPE MANGO

1 TEASPOON CASTER (SUPERFINE) SUGAR

1 TABLESPOON LIME JUICE

2 TEASPOONS FISH SAUCE

2 SMALL RED CHILLIES, FINELY CHOPPED

1 TABLESPOON CHOPPED CORIANDER (CILANTRO) LEAVES

FRESHLY GROUND BLACK PEPPER

Place the chicken pieces on a flat dish. Mix the remaining ingredients together to create a marinade, then brush all over the chicken. Cover with plastic wrap and marinate in the refrigerator for 2–3 hours, turning occasionally.

To prepare the mango salsa, peel the mango, then remove the flesh from the stone and dice finely. Put in a bowl. Make a dressing by stirring the sugar with the lime juice and fish sauce until it dissolves. Combine with the diced mango, then toss through the chilli and coriander, mixing thoroughly. Season with freshly ground black pepper.

Preheat the barbecue to medium. Place the chicken pieces on the heated, oiled barbecue plate and close the hood or cover the meat with a lid. Cook the chicken for 15 minutes, rotating regularly. Turn the chicken over and cover again. Cook for a further 15 minutes, rotating the chicken 2–3 times. Remove the lid, baste well and continue cooking, uncovered, for a further 10 minutes.

Check the chicken is cooked down to the bone by inserting a knife into the thickest part of the thigh. The chicken is cooked when the juices run clear, with no trace of pink.

To serve, arrange the chicken pieces on a platter and spoon the mango salsa over the top.

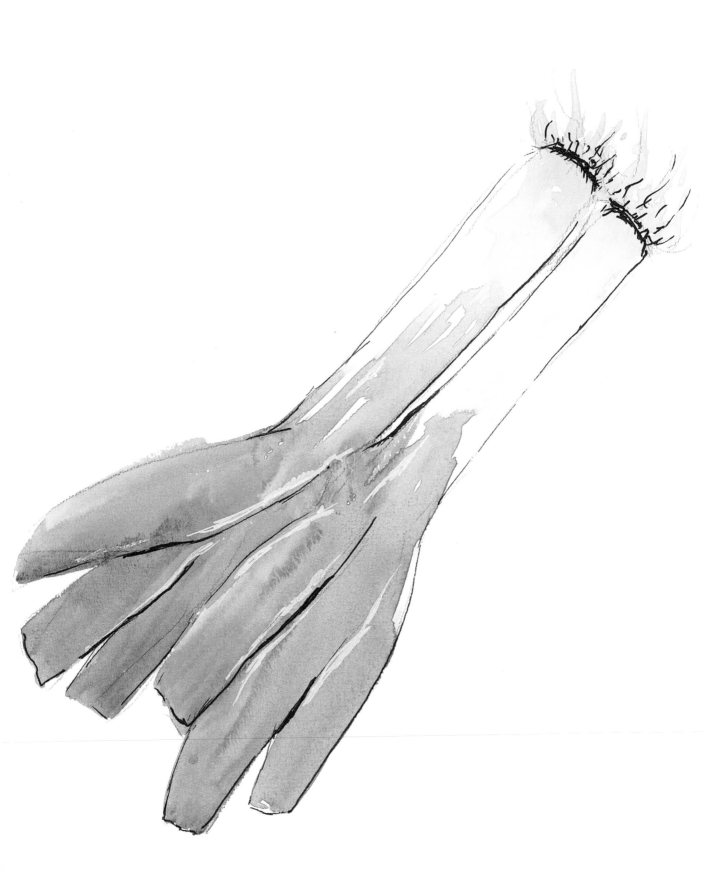

# Leek

## Risotto of cauliflower, leek and taleggio

SERVES
•
4

Heat a large heavy-based saucepan over medium heat. Add 2 tablespoons oil, 1 diced onion and 1 sliced leek, and cook for 3–4 minutes. Add 1 crushed garlic clove, then add 220 g (8 oz/1 cup) risotto rice and stir briefly. Add 125 ml (4 fl oz/½ cup) white wine and stir until absorbed. Begin adding 750 ml–1 litre (25½–34 fl oz/3–4 cups) hot vegetable or chicken stock – enough to cover the rice at first, then a ladleful at a time until absorbed, stirring well. Cook for 15–20 minutes, until the rice is just done but each grain is slightly firm in the centre. Add blanched cauliflower, a handful of grated parmesan, 100 g (3½ oz) diced taleggio (skin removed), 2 tablespoons chopped sage and 50 g (1¾ oz) diced butter. Remove from the heat and stir until the risotto is creamy and the parmesan has melted. Check the seasoning and serve.

## Scalloped potatoes with leek

SERVES
•
6

Thinly slice the white parts of 2 leeks and cook in a frying pan with a splash of olive oil until soft. Add 500 ml (17 fl oz/2 cups) milk and 250 ml (8½ fl oz/1 cup) cream, and season well with salt and freshly ground black pepper. Peel 6 large all-purpose potatoes and slice into 5 mm (¼ in) rounds. Take a deep gratin dish and brush liberally with melted butter. Add the potato slices and leeks, and pour the cream mixture over the top. Cook in a preheated 180°C (350°F) oven for 40–50 minutes, or until the potatoes are cooked and the liquid has been absorbed.

## Spiced carrot, leek and lentil soup

SERVES
•
4

Heat a large saucepan over medium heat and add a splash of oil. Add 1 diced onion, 1 thinly sliced leek, 2 diced celery stalks and 2 finely diced carrots and cook for 5 minutes, or until beginning to soften, stirring often. Add 1 crushed garlic clove, a pinch of saffron threads, 1 teaspoon each of ground cumin and coriander and 2 teaspoons harissa and cook for 2–3 minutes, until fragrant. Add 1 litre (34 fl oz/4 cups) chicken or vegetable stock and bring to the boil. Add 250 g (9 oz/1 cup) small red lentils, reduce the heat and cook for 15–20 minutes, or until the lentils are completely tender. Check the seasoning, add 2 tablespoons chopped coriander (cilantro) leaves and serve with a spoonful of Greek-style yoghurt.

# Asian greens

## Stir-fried Asian greens

SERVES
·
4

Thinly slice the stems of 200 g (7 oz) Chinese broccoli (gai larn), or any Asian greens of your choice, on an angle. Heat a splash of oil in a wok over high heat. Cook 2 crushed garlic cloves and 2 tablespoons grated ginger for 2–3 minutes, stirring often, making sure the garlic doesn't burn. Add the Chinese broccoli stems and leaves and 200 g (7 oz) chopped broccolini and toss for 1–2 minutes. Add 3 tablespoons chicken stock or water and cover with a lid. Cook for 3–4 minutes, tossing occasionally to ensure the greens cook evenly. Remove the lid and season with soy sauce.

## Soy and ginger salmon

SERVES
·
4

Put 4 salmon fillets in a shallow dish. Mix together 2 tablespoons soy sauce, 1 tablespoon grated ginger, 1 seeded and finely chopped small red chilli, 1 tablespoon oil and freshly ground black pepper. Pour the marinade over the fish and leave, covered, in the refrigerator for at least 20 minutes, but no longer than 4 hours. Remove the fish from the marinade. Cook the salmon on a medium–hot barbecue for 4 minutes on each side. Make a simple Asian-style salad by mixing 200 g (7 oz) baby bok choy (pak choy) with a handful of bean sprouts, coriander (cilantro) leaves and 4 sliced spring onions (scallions). Dress lightly with a combination of soy sauce and sesame oil.

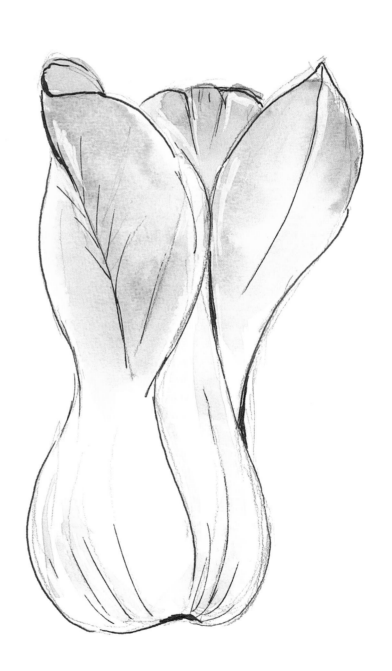

# Pork and mushroom san choy bau

San choy bau is a stunning Chinese dish that becomes even better with the addition of fresh mushrooms—try a mixture of shiitake, oyster and Swiss browns. Traditionally it uses iceberg lettuce, but is equally good with baby cos as a convenient alternative. They are very quick to make and offer fun hands-on dining as everyone gets stuck into filling their own lettuce cups. SERVES • 4–6

2 BABY COS (ROMAINE) LETTUCES

1–2 TABLESPOONS OIL

2 GARLIC CLOVES, CRUSHED

2 TEASPOONS GRATED GINGER

2 SMALL RED CHILLIES, SEEDED AND FINELY CHOPPED

200 G (7 OZ) MUSHROOMS, THINLY SLICED

500 G (1 LB 2 OZ) MINCED (GROUND) PORK

2 TABLESPOONS CHINESE RICE WINE

SOY SAUCE, TO TASTE

4 SPRING ONIONS (SCALLIONS), THINLY SLICED

Peel whole leaves away from the lettuce, wash and drain well and lay them out on a large platter.

Heat a wok over medium–high heat. Add the oil, followed immediately by the garlic, ginger and chilli. Stir well and cook until fragrant.

Add the mushrooms and stir-fry for 30 seconds. Add the minced pork and stir well for 2–3 minutes, or until the meat is cooked through. Add the Chinese rice wine and soy sauce to taste. Reduce the heat to low and simmer the mixture for 5 minutes.

Spoon the pork and mushroom mixture into the lettuce cups, add a little sliced spring onion and serve.

# Tandoori beef skewers with salsa and mint yoghurt

Charred, spiced beef skewers, tangy salsa and cooling mint yoghurt combine to make this simple yet flavoursome spring dinner. Serve with naan bread for mopping up the juices. SERVES • 4

250 G (9 OZ/1 CUP) PLAIN YOGHURT

2 TEASPOONS GROUND TURMERIC

1 TEASPOON PAPRIKA

½ TEASPOON CHILLI POWDER

1 TEASPOON GARAM MASALA

½ TEASPOON GROUND CARDAMOM

PINCH OF SAFFRON THREADS

1 TABLESPOON LEMON JUICE

500 G (1 LB 2 OZ) BEEF, SUCH AS RUMP, SCOTCH OR PORTERHOUSE, DICED

WARM NAAN BREAD, TO SERVE

**SALSA**

2 TOMATOES, DICED

1 LEBANESE (SHORT) CUCUMBER, DICED

2 SPRING ONIONS (SCALLIONS), SLICED

1 TABLESPOON CHOPPED CORIANDER (CILANTRO) LEAVES

1 TABLESPOON LIME JUICE

1 TABLESPOON OLIVE OIL

SALT AND FRESHLY GROUND BLACK PEPPER

**MINT YOGHURT**

250 G (9 OZ/1 CUP) PLAIN YOGHURT

1 TABLESPOON CHOPPED MINT

1 TABLESPOON OLIVE OIL

SALT AND FRESHLY GROUND BLACK PEPPER

Combine the yoghurt, turmeric, paprika, chilli powder, garam masala, cardamom, saffron and lemon juice in a large bowl. Add the beef, stir to coat well and refrigerate for at least 20 minutes.

Meanwhile, to make the salsa, combine the ingredients in a bowl and season with salt and freshly ground black pepper to taste. Set aside.

To make the mint yoghurt, combine the ingredients in a bowl and season to taste. Set aside.

Thread 4 or 5 pieces of beef onto separate skewers. Barbecue the skewers over medium heat for 12 minutes, turning 3 or 4 times, until cooked to medium.

Serve the cooked skewers in warm naan bread with the salsa and mint yoghurt.

# Rhubarb

## Rhubarb and cinnamon muffins

MAKES
•
10

Mix together 200 g (7 oz/1⅓ cups) self-raising flour, 1 teaspoon ground cinnamon and 115 g (4 oz/½ cup) caster (superfine) sugar in a large bowl. In a separate bowl mix together 60 g (2 oz) melted butter, 1 egg, 125 g (4½ oz/½ cup) plain yoghurt and 125 ml (4 fl oz/½ cup) milk. Add the wet mix to the dry mix and whisk until a smooth batter forms. Thinly slice 3 rhubarb stalks and fold through the muffin mix. Spoon the muffin batter into ten greased 125 ml (4 fl oz/½ cup) muffin tins. Bake in a preheated 180°C (350°F) oven for 20–25 minutes, until risen and golden brown.

## Rosewater-poached rhubarb with sweet labne

SERVES
•
4

Make the sweet labne by combining 375 g (13 oz/1½ cups) plain yoghurt, ½ teaspoon ground cardamom and 1 tablespoon icing (confectioners') sugar. Set a sieve over a bowl and line with a clean cloth. Spoon the yoghurt into the sieve, cover and refrigerate for at least 4 hours. Cook 750 ml (25½ fl oz/3 cups) water, 115 g (4 oz/½ cup) caster (superfine) sugar and 2 tablespoons rosewater in a large saucepan over low heat until the sugar dissolves. Bring to the boil. Cut 8 rhubarb stalks into 3 cm (1¼ in) lengths and add to the poaching liquid. Cook gently; you want the rhubarb to retain its shape. Remove the rhubarb and set aside. Return the syrup to the heat and cook until reduced by half. Serve the rhubarb with the sweet labne, a drizzle of the cool poaching liquid, chopped pistachios and rose petals.

## Upside-down rhubarb cake

SERVES
•
6–8

Cut 400 g (14 oz) rhubarb stalks into 4 cm (1½ in) lengths. Grease and line a 22 cm (8¾ in) springform cake tin with baking paper and arrange a single layer of rhubarb pieces on the base. Sprinkle brown sugar over and then drizzle with melted butter. Dice the remaining rhubarb and set aside. Cream 250 g (9 oz) softened diced butter and 230 g (8 oz/1 cup) caster (superfine) sugar until pale and fluffy. Add 3 eggs, one at a time, fully incorporating after each addition. Add 1 teaspoon natural vanilla extract and 225 g (8 oz/1½ cups) self-raising flour. Mix until well combined. Add the diced rhubarb to the batter, then spoon the cake mixture on top of the rhubarb in the tin. Place the tin on a lined baking tray in case of leaks, and bake in a preheated 180°C (350°F) oven for 40 minutes, or until a skewer inserted into the cake comes out clean. To serve, turn the cake upside down onto a serving plate then remove the springform tin.

# Rhubarb pound cake

Studded with tart rhubarb, this is a heavy, dense cake in the most satisfying of ways. It's perfect with a cup of tea. SERVES • 6–8

365 G (13 OZ) CASTER (SUPERFINE) SUGAR

250 G (9 OZ) RHUBARB STALKS, CUT INTO 2 CM (¾ IN) PIECES

250 G (9 OZ) BUTTER, SOFTENED

4 EGGS

250 G (9 OZ/1⅔ CUPS) SELF-RAISING FLOUR

ICING (CONFECTIONERS') SUGAR, FOR DUSTING

Preheat the oven to 180°C (350°F). Grease and line a 22 cm (8¾ in) round cake tin.

Combine 115 g (4 oz/½ cup) of the caster sugar with 250 ml (8½ fl oz/1 cup) water in a saucepan and bring to the boil over high heat. Reduce the heat, add the rhubarb and cook for 3–4 minutes, stirring occasionally, until the rhubarb is just soft. Remove the rhubarb and allow to cool before using.

Cream the butter and remaining caster sugar in a bowl until light and fluffy. Add the eggs, one at a time, allowing each one to be incorporated before adding the next. Carefully fold through the self-raising flour.

Gently combine the poached rhubarb, setting aside a few pieces for the top of the cake.

Pour the batter into the prepared tin. Top with the reserved rhubarb and bake for 40 minutes, or until the cake is cooked through. Dust with icing sugar to serve.

# Chocolate and passionfruit mousse

A good chocolate mousse is a joy to behold—and to eat, of course. This chocolate mousse tastes delicious, is incredibly simple to make, and happily adapts to having fragrant and tangy passionfruit added to it. Use the best quality chocolate you can find.

SERVES • 8

200 G (7 OZ) CHOPPED GOOD-QUALITY DARK CHOCOLATE

3 EGGS, SEPARATED

250 ML (8½ FL OZ/1 CUP) WHIPPING CREAM

6 PASSIONFRUIT, PULP STRAINED TO REMOVE THE SEEDS, PLUS EXTRA PASSIONFRUIT PULP TO TOP

Melt the chocolate by placing it in a bowl over a saucepan of simmering water or in a microwave on low for 1–2 minutes. Leave to cool slightly.

Whisk the egg whites in a bowl until soft peaks form. In a separate bowl, whip the cream until thickened.

Gently whisk the egg yolks into the melted chocolate. Add a spoonful of cream and a spoonful of egg white and fold them in; this will allow the mixture to stay aerated. Gently fold in the remaining egg whites and cream, plus the strained passionfruit pulp.

Spoon into a serving dish or individual bowls or glasses and allow to set for 2–3 hours or overnight. Serve the mousse with a little passionfruit pulp on top.

# Pineapple

## Upside-down pineapple cake

Preheat the oven to 180°C (350°F), and grease and line a 23 cm (9 in) round cake tin with baking paper. Peel and core 1 pineapple and cut into slices. Arrange a layer of slices in the base of the tin. Dice the remaining pineapple and set aside. Sprinkle 75 g (2¾ oz/⅓ cup) raw (demerara) sugar over the pineapple slices then drizzle with 4 tablespoons melted butter. Cream 100 g (3½ oz) butter and 230 g (8 oz/1 cup) caster (superfine) sugar until pale and fluffy, then beat in 3 eggs, one at a time, fully incorporating after each addition. Add 1 teaspoon natural vanilla extract and 225 g (8 oz/1½ cups) self-raising flour, and mix until well combined. Stir in the diced pineapple, then spoon the cake mixture into the tin. Bake in the oven for 40 minutes, or until a skewer inserted into the cake comes out clean. Invert onto a wire rack.

## Pineapple and cinnamon relish

Peel, core and finely dice 1 pineapple. Put it in a large saucepan with 200 g (7 oz) soft brown sugar, 125 ml (4 fl oz/½ cup) cider vinegar, ½ diced red capsicum (bell pepper), 1 diced onion, 1 pinch mixed spice, ½ teaspoon ground cinnamon and ½ teaspoon sweet paprika. Bring to the boil, then reduce the heat and cook for 30 minutes, stirring often, until thick. Add water if it looks dry. Pour into sterilised jars and leave to stand for 4 weeks to allow the flavours to develop.

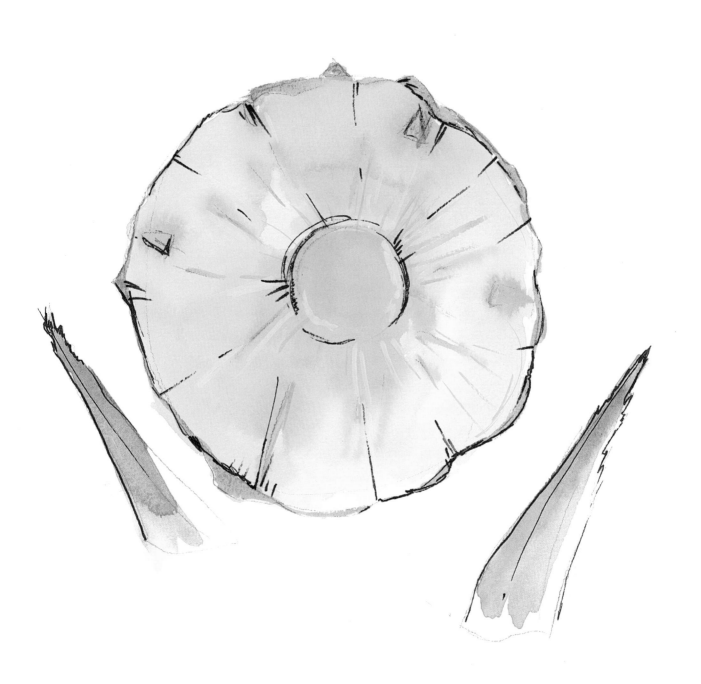

# Dulce de leche and banana meringues with salted praline

The sweetness of the pavlova combined with the salty praline is almost perfect – just add ripe bananas and you have a new Australian classic. **MAKES** • 12 MERINGUES

395 G (14 OZ) TIN SWEETENED CONDENSED MILK

4 EGG WHITES

345 G (12 OZ/1½ CUPS) CASTER (SUPERFINE) SUGAR

1 TEASPOON NATURAL VANILLA EXTRACT

1 TABLESPOON CORNFLOUR (CORNSTARCH)

1½ TEASPOONS WHITE VINEGAR

WHIPPED CREAM, FOR TOPPING

4 BANANAS, SLICED

**SALTED PRALINE**

80 G (2¾ OZ/⅓ CUP) CASTER (SUPERFINE) SUGAR

½ TEASPOON SALT

80 G (2¾ OZ/1⅓ CUPS) BLANCHED ALMONDS, TOASTED

To make the salted praline, heat the sugar and 2 tablespoons water in a small saucepan over low heat. Once the sugar has dissolved, increase the heat and bring to the boil. Swirl the syrup – do not stir – to prevent sugar crystals from forming, and cook until it becomes a light brown colour. Remove from the heat and stir in the salt and toasted almonds. Pour onto a lightly oiled baking tray and allow to set completely. Remove the cool praline from the tray, chop into bite-sized pieces and set aside.

To make the dulce de leche, put the unopened tin of condensed milk in a saucepan and cover with water. Bring to the boil, then reduce the heat and simmer for 2 hours, topping up with water if needed to ensure the tin is fully submerged at all times. Remove the tin from the water and allow to cool before opening.

Preheat the oven to 180°C (350°F). Line a baking tray with baking paper. Beat the egg whites until stiff peaks form. Add the sugar, a third at a time, incorporating well after each addition so you end up with a thick, glossy meringue. Gently fold in the vanilla, cornflour and vinegar.

Spoon 12 individual meringue rounds onto the prepared baking tray. Put in the oven and immediately reduce the temperature to 120°C (250°F) before baking for 25 minutes. Turn the oven off and let the meringues cool inside the oven.

Transfer the meringues to individual serving plates, top with whipped cream and add sliced bananas. Warm the dulce de leche slightly and drizzle over the top, then scatter with the salted praline. Serve immediately.

# Blood orange

## Blood orange baby cakes

MAKES
•
18

Boil 2 blood oranges in enough water to cover in a saucepan for 30–40 minutes, or until soft. Cool, then cut into quarters and remove the pips. Purée in a food processor until smooth. Preheat the oven to 180°C (350°F) and grease 18 × 125 ml (4 fl oz/½ cup) muffin tin. Beat 5 eggs and 230 g (8 oz/1 cup) caster (superfine) sugar for 5 minutes, or until pale and doubled in volume. Combine 250 g (9 oz/2½ cups) ground almonds and 1 teaspoon baking powder. Add the almond mixture and 500 ml (17 fl oz/2 cups) of the orange purée to the beaten eggs and incorporate well. Spoon into the prepared muffin tin and bake for 20 minutes, or until a skewer inserted into the cakes comes out clean. Cool on a wire rack.

## Blood orange and orange blossom cheesecake

SERVES
•
8

Put 150 g (5½ oz) plain sweet biscuits (cookies) and 50 g (1¾ oz/⅓ cup) blanched almonds in a food processor and process to fine crumbs. Add 75 g (2¾ oz) melted butter and process briefly. Press the biscuit mix into the base of a 20 cm (8 in) springform cake tin and refrigerate for at least 20 minutes. Finely grate the zest of 3 blood oranges, put it in a bowl with 500 g (1 lb 2 oz/2 cups) cream cheese and 145 g (5 oz/⅔ cup) caster (superfine) sugar, and beat until creamy. Juice the oranges, put the juice in a saucepan and bring to the boil. Remove from the heat, add two 5 g (¼ oz) gelatine leaves and stir until dissolved. Allow to cool slightly. Add the orange mixture to the cream cheese, along with 125 ml (4 fl oz/½ cup) cream and 1 tablespoon orange-blossom water. Stir until combined. Pour on top of the biscuit base, scatter 60 g (2 oz) chopped pistachios over and chill until set.

## Blood orange, fennel, spinach and olive salad

SERVES
•
4

Using a sharp knife, remove all peel and pith from 2 blood oranges. Slice the segments from the membranes, so that each segment is free from any pith or seeds. Put them in a bowl. Squeeze any excess juice from the orange membranes into a small bowl and set aside for dressing. Remove the tough outer layer and core from 1 fennel bulb and discard. Thinly slice the fennel and combine with the orange segments, a generous amount of baby English spinach leaves and a handful of small black olives. Make dressing by mixing 1 tablespoon red wine vinegar with the reserved orange juice. Season with salt and freshly ground black pepper and add 3 tablespoons extra-virgin olive oil. Whisk to combine and dress the salad just before serving.

# Blood orange and dark chocolate trifle

While this requires a bit of effort to prepare and construct, it's time well spent. The end result is a stunning combination of colours and flavours. SERVES • 6–8

2 TABLESPOONS GRAND MARNIER

4 BLOOD ORANGES, CUT INTO SEGMENTS

300 ML (10 FL OZ) WHIPPING CREAM

GRATED DARK CHOCOLATE, FOR SERVING

**BLOOD ORANGE JELLY**

3 × 5 G (¼ OZ) GELATINE LEAVES

250 ML (8½ FL OZ/1 CUP) BLOOD ORANGE JUICE

115 G (4 OZ/½ CUP) CASTER (SUPERFINE) SUGAR

**CHOCOLATE SPONGE**

4 EGGS

115 G (4 OZ/½ CUP) CASTER (SUPERFINE) SUGAR

100 G (3½ OZ/⅔ CUP) PLAIN (ALL-PURPOSE) FLOUR

1 TABLESPOON UNSWEETENED COCOA POWDER

**CUSTARD**

2 EGG YOLKS

3 TABLESPOONS CASTER (SUPERFINE) SUGAR

1 TABLESPOON PLAIN (ALL-PURPOSE) FLOUR

500 ML (17 FL OZ/2 CUPS) MILK

1 TEASPOON NATURAL VANILLA EXTRACT

2 TABLESPOONS GRAND MARNIER

To make the jelly, soak the gelatine leaves in cold water for 5 minutes, or until softened. Remove from the water and squeeze gently to remove excess liquid before using. Put the juice, sugar and 325 ml (11 fl oz) water in a saucepan and bring to the boil. Remove from the heat. Add the gelatine leaves and stir until dissolved. Strain into a large glass bowl and refrigerate until set.

To make the sponge, preheat the oven to 180°C (350°F). Grease a 20 × 30 cm (8 × 12 in) baking tin and line the sides and base with baking paper. Beat the eggs and sugar together until very thick and light. Sift the flour and cocoa powder and carefully fold into the egg mixture, then spoon into the prepared tin. Cook for 15–20 minutes. Test the cake by pressing the centre lightly with your fingertips; it should feel firm and bounce back when pressed. When cooked, remove from the tin and allow the cake to cool on a wire rack.

To make the custard, beat the egg yolks and sugar together until pale, then stir in the flour until smooth. Put the milk and vanilla in a saucepan and bring to the boil. Whisk the hot milk into the egg mixture, then pour into a clean saucepan. Cook the custard over low heat and stir constantly as it comes to the boil and thickens. Remove from the heat and add the Grand Marnier. Set aside to cool.

To assemble the trifle, lay slices of the sponge over the top of the jelly and sprinkle the Grand Marnier over the top. Scatter the orange segments over the top of the sponge, reserving some for garnish. Spoon the custard over the sponge and fruit, and put in the refrigerator to set.

When ready to serve, whip the cream and layer on top of the trifle, garnishing with the reserved blood orange segments and a little grated chocolate.

# Ruby grapefruit

## Quinoa tabouleh with pink grapefruit

SERVES
•
4–6 AS A
SIDE DISH

Bring 500 ml (17 fl oz/2 cups) vegetable stock or water to the boil in a saucepan with 200 g (7 oz/1 cup) quinoa and a pinch of salt. Cover and simmer over low heat for 15 minutes, or until all the liquid is absorbed. Rest, still covered, for 5 minutes, then spoon into a bowl and fluff with a fork. Remove the segments from 2 pink grapefruits, reserving the juice, and add the segments to the quinoa along with 60 g (2 oz/½ cup) roasted sunflower kernels, 2 finely diced celery stalks, 50 g (1¾ oz/⅓ cup) toasted almonds, 50 g (1¾ oz/⅓ cup) toasted pistachios, 2 tablespoons chopped mint and a handful of flat-leaf (Italian) parsley. Season well with salt and freshly ground black pepper, and drizzle with extra-virgin olive oil and 1 tablespoon reserved grapefruit juice. Toss to combine. Great with pan-fried fish.

## Spring fruit salad with rosewater syrup

SERVES
•
4–6

Put 250 ml (8½ fl oz/1 cup) water and 165 g (6 oz/¾ cup) sugar in a saucepan. Add a few saffron threads and cardamom pods. Heat until the sugar dissolves. Remove from the heat and allow to cool for 5 minutes. Add 2 teaspoons rosewater plus the juice of 1 lime. Prepare a fruit salad with the most beautiful spring produce: try segments of oranges and pink grapefruit, ripe strawberries and slices of mango and pineapple. Combine in a deep bowl and drizzle with the rosewater syrup. Allow to marinate for 2 hours, stirring occasionally. Serve with a dollop of Greek-style yoghurt.

# Index

Published in 2016 by Hardie Grant Books

Hardie Grant Books (Australia)
Ground Floor, Building 1
658 Church Street
Richmond, Victoria 3121
www.hardiegrant.com.au

Hardie Grant Books (UK)
5th & 6th Floors
52-54 Southwark Street
London SE1 1UN
www.hardiegrant.co.uk

A Cataloguing-in-Publication entry is available from the catalogue of the National Library of Australia at www.nla.gov.au

Harvest
ISBN 978 1 74379 011 3

Project Editor: Simon Davis
Editor: Paul McNally
Design Manager: Vaughan Mossop
Designer, Photographer and Illustrator: Emilie Guelpa
Production Manager: Todd Rechner

Recipe text by Allan Campion and Michele Curtis

Colour reproduction by Splitting Image Colour Studio
Printed in China by 1010 Printing International Limited